Directions for Directing

Directions for Directing: Theatre and Method lays out contemporary concepts of directing practice and examines specific techniques of approaching scripts, actors, and the stage. Addressed to both young and experienced directors but also to the broader community of theatre practitioners, scholars, and dedicated theatre goers, the book sheds light on the director's multiplicity of roles throughout the life of a play—from the moment of its conception to opening night—and explores the director's processes of inspiration, interpretation, communication, and leadership. From organizing auditions and making casting choices to decoding complex dramaturgical texts and motivating actors, *Directions for Directing* offers practical advice and features detailed Workbook sections on how to navigate such a fascinating discipline. A companion website explores the work of international practitioners of different backgrounds who operate within various institutions, companies, and budgets, providing readers with a wide range of perspectives and methodologies.

Avra Sidiropoulou is Assistant Professor at the MA program in Theatre Studies at the Open University of Cyprus. Her research focuses on the theory, practice, and ethics of contemporary directing. She is the Artistic Director of the Athens-based Persona Theatre Company and has produced work internationally.

Directions for Directing

Theatre and Method

Avra Sidiropoulou

Routledge
Taylor & Francis Group

NEW YORK AND LONDON

First published 2019
by Routledge
711 Third Avenue, New York, NY 10017

and by Routledge
2 Park Square, Milton Park, Abingdon, Oxon, OX14 4RN

Routledge is an imprint of the Taylor & Francis Group, an informa business

Library of Congress Cataloging-in-Publication Data
Names: Sidiropoulou, Avra, 1972– author.
Title: Directions for directing: theatre and method /
Avra Sidiropoulou.
Description: New York, NY: Routledge, 2019. |
Includes bibliographical references and index.
Identifiers: LCCN 2018018200 | ISBN 9780415789271
(hardback: alk. paper) | ISBN 9780415789288
(paperback: alk. paper) | ISBN 9781315222905 (ebook)
Subjects: LCSH: Theater—Production and direction.
Classification: LCC PN2053 .S453 2019 |
DDC 792.02/33—dc23
LC record available at https://lccn.loc.gov/2018018200

ISBN: 978-0-415-78927-1 (hbk)
ISBN: 978-0-415-78928-8 (pbk)
ISBN: 978-1-315-22290-5 (ebk)

Typeset in Sabon
by codeMantra

Visit the companion website: www.routledge.com/cw/sidiropoulou

To Nikiforos always, and now to Sophocles

Contents

Figures

Acknowledgments

This book would not have been possible without the support of several talented and committed friends and colleagues. I would like to thank Stacey Walker, my editor at Routledge, for believing and investing in the project, and the assistant editor, Lucia Accorsi, for her dedication and efficiency throughout the process. Many thanks to my production editor, Paige Force, for putting it all together.

Part of my research was undertaken at the Graduate Center of the City University of New York, where I was a Visiting Scholar in 2016. Heartfelt thanks to Frank Hentschker, Director of the Martin E. Segal Centre, for making me feel at home within that vibrant community of academics and artists. Also to the Faculty members Professor Marvin Carlson and Professor Peter Eckersall for sharing their valuable insights on the contemporary theatre scene internationally. While in New York, I had the opportunity to speak with various theatre artists, holding conversations that have affected my perception of directing and that have, in one way or another, featured here. I am grateful to John Collins, Artistic Director of Elevator Repair Service, who kindly agreed to share his creative process in the Web Companion section of the book. Special thanks to Charles Mee, whose writing has always been of great inspiration, and to Anne Bogart for her valuable intuitions.

This project was greatly assisted by the opportunities I have had to teach and conduct practical workshops in different parts of the world in order to test empirically some of the exercises that are part and parcel of the book as well as to explore alternative forms of practice. I am thankful to the Japan Foundation for the generous grant that allowed me to spend time as a visiting fellow at the University of Tokyo and to Professor Tadashi Uchino for exposing me to the distinct methodologies of Japanese theatre. I am also indebted to Jay Scheib, stage director and Head of the Music and Theater Arts Department at the Massachusetts Institute of Technology, for inviting me over as a Visiting Researcher. Also to Dr. George Rodosthenous at the University of Leeds for giving me the opportunity to lecture and work with directing students at the

School of Performance and Creative Industries, and for always being there with sound advice and a wealth of information on the latest in British directing—he is a great source. Many thanks to Dr. Eirini Nedelkopoulou for organizing targeted directing workshops at the School of Performance & Media Production at York St John's University and for being such an intelligent interlocutor.

The Web Companion section that accompanies the book has brought together the expertise and commitment of several artists whose work I admire. They have all agreed to share their ideas on camera, even under strained conditions. The geographical distance separating us, if anything, has added to the value of intercultural collaboration. Lighting designer Maria Cristina Fusté, a Puerto Rican artist based in New York; the actor-director Kate Mueth of Neo-Political Cow Girls at the Hamptons; Athens-based set designer and scholar Athena Stourna; Vanessa Christodoulou, graduate of the MA Program in Theatre Studies at the Open University of Cyprus; and performer-director-dramaturg Miranda Manasiadis and choreographer Malia Johnston of Movement of the Human, both based in New Zealand, have all made this live component truly rich. Besides Elevator Repair Service's John Collins, director-playwright Oriza Hirata of Tokyo's Seinendan and Lars Romann Engel, director of Helsinore-based HamletScenen, have generously shared their thoughts on specific aspects of the directing art and theatre practice, in general. I would like to warmly thank Dr. Anne Sophie Refskou from Surrey University for arranging the interview with Lars Engel in Denmark. And, of course, Dr. Ana Contreras at the Real Escuela Superior de Arte Dramatico de Madrid in Spain for arranging directing workshops with the students, whose work is also present here.

Many, many thanks to my close friends Alisa Regas and Ilker Oztop in New York for being so hospitable during my research time there.

Special thanks to graphic designer Babis Melikidis for helping realize the artlog. Warmest thanks to photographer Michael Demetrius for the front cover image and to Miranda Manasiadis, Mikaela Liakata, Lena Gini, Julia Kogkou, Effi Eglezaki, Vanias Apergis, and Giannis Tsoumarakis, who worked on the *Phaedra—I* workshop in Athens in 2017.

There is simply no easy way to express my gratitude to Emy Tzavra-Bulloch, an experienced filmmaker and video editor, for endorsing the book's Web Companion with such fierce dedication and resourcefulness. I do not think I would have pulled through without her great sense of responsibility, ingenuity, and humor.

I would like to thank my parents, Freideriki and Panagiotis, and my sister, Dr. Chryssi Sidiropoulou, for their lifelong encouragement, and my two sons, Nikiforos and Sophocles, for being patient and strong. And, most of all, Dimitris, for his insightful suggestions on the manuscript and for his love, companionship, and faith in me.

There are so many other people whose practical, technical, scholarly, or emotional support has been really instrumental to my work and whose names do not appear in the list. Thank you for being there. Finally, a heartfelt thanks to all the great theatre artists in all parts of the world, whose work has inspired this book.

Introduction

Why Directing? Why Directions?

We all carry a director in us. In our family routines, our workplace, our social interactions, conversations with friends, mundane dealings with the outside world, or during those rare moments of solitary clarity, when our sharp focus on reality begins to merge with softer forms of perception, we tend to direct our lives, filtering facts that have already occurred or recalibrating thoughts toward imaginary possibilities. Directors are authors of culture, privileged with freedom, authority and a limitless power to interpret the world and its dictums. A good director is a fearless director who remains consistent and relentless to the mission of realizing a vision, no matter how utterly illogical it may appear to others. The allure of the directing profession is no accident: directing is primarily about creating new realities and, as such, it is inextricably linked to reinvention and redefinition.

Many argue that directing is basically about instinct, and therefore, it cannot be taught. I tend to disagree. Much though directing is about instinct, it is also about technique, form, control of the stage, developing your own language, and making informed choices. All these things are learnt gradually, be it in a formal educational context or in the context of practice. The growing number of MA and MFA directing courses, together with the proliferation of young theatre companies worldwide make pressing demands for up-to-date educational materials that analyze the theory and practice of the art through a combined application of traditional and innovative methodologies and rehearsal strategies. Besides, there is an extraordinary number of practitioners (including actors, writers, and designers) who have received no formal training within an academic or conservatoire setting and who could benefit from a study that details the fundamentals of theatre making—both regarding theoretical underpinnings and practical applications.

Directions for Directing is an acknowledgment of the need to describe the methodology of directing, how an original vision is born and developed to a full production. It is intended as a useful guide for prioritizing the mental and experiential steps this process involves and as a tool of teaching a discipline that is both complex and elusive. In its synthetic approach, it comes to fill a void in theatre scholarship, theorizing on the motivations that make directors create, and laying out a model of work that sets the consecutive stages of the director's individual and collaborative process clearly and concisely. All through, it tries to remain in keeping with the dual nature of directing: on the one hand as an aesthetic and philosophical pursuit which needs to be cultivated, and on the other, as an aspect of theatre that relies on a series of practical skills and strategies that can be taught. More than anything, it is as much about the art of directing as it is about theatre and its method.

The book is, therefore, an attempt, means of communication, as well as instruction, to tap into those notions of the art that are a series of abstract considerations but also a handling of different skills—organizational, interpersonal, and technical. Moreover, it aims to inspire alternative angles through which to perceive and express the world. As such, it builds on a vocabulary that directors, actors, designers, producers, and regular theatregoers may use, while discussing several aspects of theatre practice. Citing relevant instances and proposing creative (re)solutions for the gestation period of preparation and the actual rehearsals, it is aimed not just to the director (young, amateur, or experienced) but also very much so to the broader community of actors, dramaturgs, set, costume, lighting, video and sound designers, and choreographers; in fact, to anyone directly or indirectly involved in the theatre.

Examples from the work methodologies of established artists internationally serve to bring home the idea that directing is an extremely generous, virtually inexhaustible art; needless to say, the inclusion of some directors at the expense of a multitude of others is by no means an indication of lack of extraordinary talent in the profession. Moreover, excerpts from individual plays are also brought in for the reader to make immediate connections between the theoretical observations and their hands-on application. In general, most of the examples I used in order to make an illustration come alive and ensure its effectiveness are drawn from popular plays. While I am aware of the immense value of lesser-known experimental play scripts, the existing plays provide easy reference and direct access to analysis both in the main body of the book and in the Workbook sections. That said, my discussion of seminal aspects of directing such as text and scenography includes updated perspectives from contemporary forms of theatre making: visual and media textualities and the adventurous practices of site-specific and immersive theatre are discussed alongside more "traditional" elements of the theatre, as are story, character, dialogue, and actions.

Structurally, the book focuses on the fundamental tenets that define a director's work from the initial moment of inspiration to preparation to rehearsals to opening night, featuring a dual focus on critical concepts, on the one hand, and practical applications utilizing exercises, on the other. The division into six chapters roughly follows the work of a director from the play's conception through to the moment a performance is delivered to an audience. The different sections of the book are organized in such a way as to suggest the director's multiplicity of roles and the complexity of the directing profession. Therefore, the first three chapters (Chapter 1. "Inspiration", Chapter 2. "Interpretation", and Chapter 3. "Method, Leadership, Collaboration") analyze the mental steps that inform the director's understanding of a play, but also discuss an array of production choices in which the director engages before and during rehearsal. Among other things, they discuss the sources of directorial inspiration, strategies for motivating actors and spectators, point of view, metaphor, and style. They also address the pragmatics of such immediate matters as making casting and venue choices, organizing auditions and rehearsals and facilitating a collaborative spirit, while exhibiting a strong sense of leadership. The remaining three chapters (Chapter 4. "Director and Text(uality)," Chapter 5. "Director and Stage," and Chapter 6. "Director and Actor") concentrate on the director's work with the text, the stage, and the actor, by means of theory, examples, and recorded analyses of select directing strategies. They detail the process of decoding complex dramaturgical coordinates and explore the director's manipulation of space and sound as well as the dialogue between the director and the design team, and finally the fascinating relationship between director and actor. Each section is accompanied by a "Workbook," which aims to solidify these concepts further into tangible practice. By no means exhaustive or applicable in every rehearsal context, the exercises are meant to be *suggestions* for directing students and for practicing directors.

An integral and vital innovation of the book is the Web Companion. Its sections feature the work of international, mostly younger generation practitioners of different backgrounds who operate within various institutions, companies, or budgets. These artists include directors (John Collins of award-winning, New York City-based Elevator Repair Service, Oriza Hirata of Tokyo-based Seinendan, and Lars Lars Romann Engel of Helsinore-based HamletScenen) and actors (Kate Mueth of Neo-Political Cowgirls, based in the Hamptons, New York, and New Zealand-based Miranda Manasiadis). Set and lighting designers (Athens-based Athena Stourna and New York City-based Maria Cristina Fusté) discuss their methodology and process of collaborating with the director. Last but not least, directing students from RESAD, the renowned academy of drama in Madrid, and Athens-based Vanessa Christodoulou share their work and their thoughts on whether directing can be taught and on what makes for a valuable directing education.

In the final analysis, the book envisions the practicalities of economy and style. And while *Directions for Directing* is primarily addressed to directors, actors, playwrights, and other theatre artists, one should never ignore the numerous and ever supportive theatre aficionados who wish to know more about the making of a play and the development of a form, following the journey of an art product throughout its tumultuous lifespan. In this light, the book is a methodology of staging plays answering to the fundamental questions of why, where, when, and how a text can be rendered performance, once an idea strikes you and the skin of imagination is torn open. It is a small token of appreciation to every theatre-loving person, another gateway to the mysteries of the director's art, the codes, and formulas of the stage.

Chapter 1

Inspiration

Becoming Inspired

Connection and Choice

As a director, you operate on inspiration—the fuel that gets your engine going. You'll find it in every creative act, an indispensable element without which few works of art can ever feel complete. All vigor, claimed American transcendentalist poet and philosopher Ralph Emerson, is contagious, and when we see creation, we also begin to create. Each inspired vision of the world represented onstage, can, in some way or another, lead both artists and spectators to uplifting physical, psychological, or mental actions. First and foremost, however, feeling inspired is a prerequisite for any fulfilling interaction between a director and a theatre company: not only a profoundly personal but also a contagious affair, which combines the past of your background and training, the present of rehearsal work, and the future of sharing a performance with an audience. In the world of directing, inspiration usually comes across as a sincere instinctual attachment to an idea; an image; a sound; a person; or a sensory, emotional, or intellectual stimulus, which activates the imagination, generating a mood for reflection and a desire for expression and participation. A rare approximation of an ideal and a state of clarity and engagement, it is both a blessing and a necessity. Essentially, inspiration can be described in terms of a discovery: a dormant thought, feeling, or response suddenly reemerges, preparing us to meet the world in all its turmoil.

For directors and audiences alike, performances can be powerful triggers of inspiration. They invite us to think, participate, share, play, empathize, and imagine. Directors are usually attracted to particular genres, texts, themes, and processes, a connection that is essential for artistic growth. The decision to embark on a project varies according to factors determined by personality, life circumstances, education, and training. Complex needs further inform the choice of material, and as a result, different decisions describe and generate different work methodologies and styles, approaches to text and to form, as well as hierarchies of meaning-making. The one thing, however, that is common in most creative practices is the artists' strong affinity to their source. Such a bond usually drives art that is nothing short of necessary and that appears inevitable.

> Which are a director's sources of inspiration?

> What makes some directors more inspiring than others?

> Is an inspired director by definition inspirational?

> Can inspiration be communicated?

Some of the aforementioned questions, which keep resurfacing in many discussions on directing, are naturally rhetorical. There are no recipes or manuals for readily available inspiration circulating freely among theatre makers. These queries do, however, serve a dual function: they help us think about inspiration as an *impulse*—something that is instantaneous and irresistible—and a *process* that can be communicated and cultivated. Jerzy Grotowski's observation sums it up nicely: "The director's purpose is to create a condition which leads another to a new experience; a thousand times it won't work, but once it will, and that once is essential" (qtd in Benedetti 1985, 129).

Love and Meaningfulness

In the case of preexisting plays—as opposed to devised or nonverbal material—directors relate to the text for various reasons and through different mediums. You may, for instance, enjoy a play's intricate structure, the unexpected manipulation of dramatic form, the freshness of ideas, or the complexity of the characters. Yet the original *connection* you experience pierces through the transparency of form toward something much more intuitive. Whether or not you are intrigued by the suspenseful plot, political acumen, density of imagery, or authentic feel of dialogue, sooner or later, you will need to address the text's *meaningfulness*, a sense of urgency and an emphasis on whatever feels relevant at a particular moment in time. In point of fact, directing forces you to step out of your comfort zone and reflect on how history, culture, and the global scope of contemporary society not only influence your life but also affect everybody around you. Striving for meaningfulness has as much to do with asking the big human questions as with being able to articulate why a specific text must be delivered to an audience now. In this sense, inspiration seems to be a medium for (re)discovering meaning.

As readers who flip through the pages of a play script for the first time, we unconsciously expect a revelation. We crave to be surprised, even shocked, because when that happens, we feel more alive. Bonding with a text unearths undeclared feelings, impels—almost forces—us to express ourselves. Directors, in particular, are especially sensitive to these epiphanies. Each new reading can be an opportunity for enlightenment, an opening into a range of aesthetic and emotive experiences, a possibility for wisdom and beauty, all of which can create moments of theatre that can move, instruct, and delight. Good art stimulates more good art, awakening the desire for creativity. And because texts are processed both emotionally and intellectually, it stands to reason that during the early readings, you, the director, are absorbed *dually*—both intuitively and analytically. Your initial confrontation with a play stimulates all kinds of images and impetuous, almost irrational reactions. Such responses, far from mere abstractions, are predominantly embodied. As neuroscientist Antonio Damasio argues, the essence of feelings can be described as something "you and I can see through a window that opens directly onto a continuously updated image of the structure and state of our body" (Damasio 1994, xviii). The understanding that "a feeling is the momentary 'view' of a part of [...] body landscape" (xix) may, for example, explain why our pulse quickens or our stomach tightens when we experience something that excites us.

It is during this phase that you will begin to grasp the emotional temperature of the play and form a preliminary sensory score based on the imagery and rhythm of the words on the page. Those first readings encourage you to receive everything the text emits without censoring it or testing its validity and value. This kind of engrossment may lead to useful building blocks with which you can develop your vision; it is a unique, *creative reading*, a by-proxy staging that takes place in an (virtual) intermediary field, where the universe of the play and that of the interpreter (director) come into close contact. The two worlds—alternately antagonizing and validating or complementing each other—exist in a nebulous space defined mainly by the interaction of the context provided by the written words and the director's life experience. As a result, interpretation is negotiated as an inspiration-based encounter, where meaning is produced both individually, in the mind of the director, and jointly, in the dialogue between the director, the company, and the text.

Creative Reading is an involved *lécture* that invites "stage readers" (virtual directors) to look for performative parameters in the text. Unwittingly, these lectors project their memories and speculations on their reading, not only playing back their life stories but also mentally placing themselves in specific theatre spaces and setting those stories to images, sounds, or patterns of movement. In the end, the text becomes dynamically "in-space/d" and stageable, at least in the reader's mind.

Any encounter with the text mobilizes a circuit of diverse reflections, often imparting universal knowledge expressed from unusual angles. Remaining open to this nexus of influences, you are actually inviting inspiration to enter your work. After all, it is nothing but a catalyst that helps stirring impressions to emerge out of your mental storage of life experiences. And even though a director may "periodically tidy, sort, arrange and file the contents" in the "lumber rooms" that exist in the "attics of his memory," there must always be an "untidiness," some degree of "clutter" that can "reappear spontaneously when needed" (Roose-Evans 1968, 83–4). Once revealed and addressed, the "clutter" will no longer be an unacknowledged and disposable mess but will emerge in more definite shapes and force you to get to work and create.

On occasion, directors-readers will be struck by an idea they will want to develop further, a concept that feels fresh to the moment but has somehow been constantly present in their mind. A conversation you may have overheard, a memorable scene witnessed, a piece of literature with astonishing language, and numerous other triggers are all instances of a rush of inspiration which can also affect choice. Some stories convey themes that specifically touch upon fears or desires cast aside for too long. They draw us in without notice and produce reflex responses that can be pleasurable or disturbing but are almost always significant. As a director, you are likely to have been consciously or unconsciously pulled toward plays whose contexts recall your life circumstances or those that raise questions you have a burning desire to address. Often, there is this nagging thought at the back of your head that dealing with your issues from the safety of distance can lead to a sharper awareness, a fuller recognition, a smoother recovery. To use an example: calling attention to the idea of personal responsibility, Henrik Ibsen's *Little Eyolf* (1894) tells the story of an estranged couple's (Alfred and Rita Allmer's) pain and guilt when forced to come to terms with the death of their nine-year-old child. Because of the somber subject matter and sinister tone, the play never made it to the playwright's "top-5" works. Yet Ibsen's profound treatment of loss and denial could mean a lot to those similarly afflicted, making their personal investment stronger and their response to the text potentially more discerning. Despite the distress you experience at the invocation of painful memories, subconsciously, you may be prepared to tackle such accumulated affliction vicariously.

It is no wonder that the collision of texts and people, of creative material and artists, has repeatedly been described as a *coup de foudre* (love at first sight), an immediate attraction, a condition similar to intoxication, which fires up unconscious reverberations. British director Katie Mitchell describes the sensation generated from reading a text one wants to direct as "akin to falling in love," where one may find that their "heartbeat increases and their body temperature rises" (Mitchell 2008, 8). In time, the dedicated involvement with a text—a self-ruling plexus of ideas and emotions—will feel like a deeply committed relationship. A strong attachment is necessary for endorsing any project because when you connect, the company and the audience will also connect. In contrast, the absence of engagement can be a warning sign, a kind of red flag for which you should watch out. If your original drive is weak, there is little you can do to support your longing to make captivating theatre. Directing is as much about instinct and passion as it is about cognition and method.

WORKBOOK 1.1

The Workbook section of the book has sampled a range of exercises that are meant to be a warm-up or general rehearsal tools for the director and the company of actors. Depending on the levels of experience, some exercises will serve better in a group of beginners, while others may feel more specialized or advanced. If this is a class of directing students, you can gauge the exercises' usefulness and applicability to specific teaching units. Often, examples from well-known plays are brought in to clarify their function and scope. Usually, the activities provide a model framework within which to examine the particular text (here referred to as "play of choice") that a theatre company is staging or on which a directing/drama/acting/scenography class is currently working.

Practice 1. Connecting to the Text

The following activities are meant to reveal a more personal connection to the source.

Activity 1. Identifying the Connection

> Pick up the climactic scene from your play of choice.
> Read it through, and then put it aside.

> Give it some time to "sit," and then try to summarize in one sentence the core event of the scene. The way you respond will make plain your original, instinctive approach to the text.

After determining what the scene is about, try describing it to someone else in as much detail as possible. As a director, you should ask your actors to take turns with their own sentence.

You will realize that the way each version is colored, including possible omissions or points of emphasis, has a lot to do with how actors *read themselves* into the world of the play, in general.

Activity 2. Building on the Connection

Ask your group members to discuss their involvement with the play of choice. Could they be characters in it? Have they ever been in any situation that even remotely resembles what goes on in the text? Apply the same questions to yourself, the director of the piece.

Ask your actors to change the character's name into their own and to turn the other characters' names into the names of people who play an active part in their life. Do the same thing for yourself.

Focus on the part of the play that is particularly interesting to you/them. Adjust the circumstances of the play to yours/theirs, and try to "meet" the text, stretching the story line as much as it allows you to.

You may give your play a different ending or keep it open.

You can now go back to the text and reread it.

Soon, you'll begin to find yourself behind many parts. Isolate the ones that are unusually persistent.

Pinpoint your primary connection to the play, and ask your company to identify theirs. You and your actors are now one step closer to a solid concept for the production.

Communicating Your Vision

Spreading the Disease

Negotiating between the pragmatics of production and the fleeting nature of imagination is a crucial challenge. Sometimes, the clamor of administration takes priority over the slow-burning, invisible demands of ephemeral inspiration, which can disappear just as fast as it first hits. Granted, it is rare to respond immediately to a new stimulus; it is useful, however, to recognize the function of inspiration as a call to action and a force that sets things moving, and accept that, in and of itself, inspiration instigates interpretation. In rehearsal, interest and commitment are solid venture points for exploration. Not only can inspiration reveal the less-apparent reasons why you may want to work on a particular play or a particular theme at this moment in time; it also motivates you to revise hermeneutic mechanisms of analysis and research verbal, visual, and kinetic forms that will support your original vision.

Enjoying the luxury of building autonomous, although fictional, realities that bear their own rules and can transport audiences "into states of mind rather than real places" (Rich 1985), directors typically carry enhanced privileges and responsibilities within the ensemble. The collaborative nature of theatre-making notwithstanding, you are expected to envision the entire production, draft out models of staging, provide the materials, and oversee its progress. Combining the functions of an architect, a contractor, and a construction worker, you will be held accountable for handing in a functional and enterprising building plan.

Interestingly, the manner in which theatre practice continues for the most part to layer the several stages and agents of inspiration from playwright down to spectator echoes Plato's dialogue *Ion* (380 BCE), which addresses the theme of divine poetic inspiration. In *Ion*, Socrates claims that both poet and *rhapsode* (the poet's interpreter) are conquered by a spell of divine inspiration resembling a magnet, which brings upon itself metal rings and enables them to collect upon them other magnets. The Muse initially inspires the poets, gifted individuals who have been possessed by divine enthusiasm, to subsequently inspire the rhapsodes to recite what has been communicated to them. The rhapsodes, therefore, become the "interpreters of interpreters" and, in turn, pass on their inspiration to the spectators, the last of the rings to receive the force of the original magnet, one from the other. Several centuries after Plato's time, even if, admittedly, the secret to making good theatre is also determined by the handling of prosaic considerations, a sense of "divine" agency, a strong impetus outside of the self, remains vital to securing the right circumstances for creativity and invention. Setting the mood for exploration is part of the understanding that "what is being transmitted is not simply information and what is being absorbed is individual and private" (Cole 1992, 12).

A shared artistic outlook is a crucial factor of achievement in any collaborative work. Typically, at the onset of rehearsals, directors will discuss their personal reasons for working on the play. Getting the team to rejoice in your passion heavily depends on your ability to communicate with charisma and conviction. Try to get your ideas across with transparency and show your devotion from the start so that your group can feel secure in your commitment and remain connected through and against potential misadventures during rehearsals and in the entire production run.

The director's inspired communication of directorial vision to the company helps:

> Actors to fine-tune aspects of the character they have adopted and work on a personal but consistent take on the role.

> Set designers to own the idea of the imagined space where the action will be situated and understand how the given theatre architecture works, to be in a better position to construct their own ideal home for the play.

> Costume designers to work more in-depth with the fundamental metaphor of the play, producing stylistically consistent visual concepts about each of the characters.

> Sound designers to reflect on the auditory environment of the play in order to compose the performance's soundscape.

> Choreographers to explore the physical life of the production and give performers specific movement and gestural patterns that are functional, expressive, and consistent with the directorial vision.

Long-standing ensembles, accustomed to specific directors' methodology and style, will probably respond to their creative prompts at once, without too much feedback or clarification. Other times, especially when director and company are new to each other, the courtship may be slow and even grueling, and it will take persistence, ingenuity, cajoling, seducing, and various other subtle or unabashed tactics for a flash of inspiration to travel back and forth. Still, while the company may not in the end enjoy the shocking force of your own (unmediated) original response to the material, your role as director is vital in letting interest build with time and survive what could be an uneven or tumultuous process.

Sheltering Surprise

That surprise—the core of transformation—is the DNA of theatre has been severally stated. Thankfully, adventure-proof narratives have long ceased to be the representational ideal in either dramaturgy or performance. Because transformation and magic are basic human needs, there is a great deal to benefit from by rejecting the commonplace and stepping onto less-familiar ground. This idea rings particularly true if we take into account that the ambition to interpret the world beyond the fiction of the real is innate for both artists and audiences. In fact, as much as we may fear it, there is always a sense of pleasure in being caught off-balance. To be surprising, allow for a certain degree of fearlessness to lead you into uncharted artistic territory where things begin to get uncomfortable.

> Directing is a leap into the unknown, an encounter with someone else's world, which nevertheless releases powerful personal emotions. It makes you look back into yourself. It also unwittingly points you to unexpected angles from which to experience life and express things that are significant not only to you but also to your audience.

Like actors, audiences also welcome surprises, no less because they touch upon regions of the subconscious where things imagined, fantasized, or even dreaded reside with little hope of release. We go to the theatre to revel in a world that is different from ours and to be exposed to exciting alternatives, now finally voiced. We also like to admire the sheer craftsmanship of art, the way everyday things metamorphose into sophisticated staging. Unusual choices in storytelling, imagery, movement, rhythm, sound, technology, and acting styles in performances that "resist or deny the usual channels of decoding" (Bennett 1990, 103) can change the understanding of the familiar, introducing audacious modes of awareness. As a director, you may naturally stumble through the imaginative turbulence that comes attached to different readings and staging possibilities, but, in the end, all you can do is embrace the risk. The metaphoric function of the director as a keen traveler and survivor of mighty adventures has often been raised: "Like Darwin, the director is an explorer who seeks truth in minute particulars. And like Darwin, the director is not immune from disorientation during the voyage but finds [his or her] bearings in the midst of a storm" (Cole 1992, 79).

> The stage is a place where anything seems possible through a poetic touch and where things usually "forbidden" or simply inaccessible are frequently projected in plain view.
>
> • The more unexpected the setup, the more exciting the event.
>
> • The more boldly you handle subversion and distortion, tension, and revelation, the more compelling the production can become.

In performance, you can introduce mystery and challenge by implementing structures that are independent of conventional cause-and-effect logic and by discarding explicit metaphors and descriptive iconography in favor of narrative patterns that trigger the subconscious more subtly. Sometimes, nonrealistic forms bring wonderment and epiphanies. If you bravely handle theatre semiosis—the way the elements of the stage are organized to make a statement of interpretation—your *mise-en-scène* is destined to stimulate dormant associations rather than merely illustrate the text. To bring a notable example: in the imagistic work of American visual artist and director Robert Wilson, correspondences between seemingly incompatible things are accepted as natural, while recourse to archetypical imagery is prevalent. In Wilson's and composer Philip Glass's emblematic opera *Einstein on the Beach* (1976), the production's principal visual properties, namely, a train, a trial, and a field, teem with transformative potential. An ordinary children's fixation and great fairytale stock, a cardboard train crosses slowly from right to left. The same train switches to something more sinister during a mock romantic nighttime scene of a traveling couple, during which a woman pulls out a gun on her husband. By a similar stroke of imagination, following a frenzied elevator sequence that features a young boy going up and down in a glass cubicle, Wilson's stage converts into a spaceship, made up of a three-story-high, flame-orange structure amid billowing smoke and brilliant lighting flashing on and off. The spaceship figure is one of the universals Wilson employs—clocks and compasses are also ubiquitous in the production—to bring everyone together, performers, characters, and spectators, in one single ahistorical dimension, a "multi-cultural, ethnological, archaeological *kaleidoscope*" (Lehmann 2006, 79, emphasis original). As the language of the subconscious, symbols are everybody's cognitive property, and their commanding presence onstage adds to a shared appreciation, a "spectators' own" form of partnership.

In fact, on the level of both narrative and staging, you can juxtapose or mix familiar and unfamiliar elements to an equally gripping effect. In the 1917 essay "Art as Technique," formalist literary theorist Viktor Shklovsky, instigator of the concept of "defamiliarization," would declare that the purpose of art was "to impart the sensation of things as they are perceived and not as they are known." He insisted that the process of making objects "unfamiliar" and forms "difficult" was a necessary component of the technique of art. Precisely because the purpose of art was to make one experience the "artfulness of an object," the process of perception itself was "aesthetic" and as such should be prolonged (Shklovsky 1965, 12). Being an alive and interactive art, theatre is the ideal medium for turning the most banal snapshots into compelling moments. More than anything, our sensations of pleasure and satisfaction thrive in revelation. The examples from Wilson's work suggest that a director can reframe the commonplace unpredictably to yield properties of added artistic and spiritual value. Or, as John Collins, Artistic Director of the New York-based Elevator Repair Service, claims, "If what you want to do is discover things, then put things together that don't already have a predictable relationship, try to resolve them and see what you get" (2016).

The unorthodox use of atmosphere, music, movement, and lighting heightens the audience's experience of the sublime. Recourse to visual imagery arouses sensory impact, allowing for a different kind of visceral appreciation. Think, for example, of the old-time favorites of natural elements such as water, snow, or fire, whose presence onstage has always had a magnetic effect on audiences, even at times when, as the joke has it, directors appear to have run out of ideas. While a detailed discussion on the languages of staging is part of another chapter of this book, we can never tire of acknowledging design as one of the most authoritative aspects of directing, given how much it indulges the hunger for aesthetic consummation. Darkness interrupted by streaks of lightning is just thrilling to watch. Sudden rain pelting down on a theatre set can provoke gasps of amazement. An unusual composition of bodies on different planes and levels, changing shapes and sizes all in the course of one scene, is just another fascinating occasion that only theatre can pull through with such economy and immediacy. These magical moments, however common or simple, are tokens of theatrical ingenuity, a chance for spectators to experience how reality is (momentarily) transcended.

After all, a performance is "a time set aside from daily life in which something might occur [...]. You must be available and attentive to the doors that open unexpectedly" (Bogart 2001, 75). And even if some tricks may betray much more sophisticated directorial choices than others, the slightest suggestion of "magic" onstage may be enough to win the audience's gratitude. Just as much, the actors', designers', and spectators' interpretation can be unlocked as soon as they welcome disorientation and lack of certainty as a positive thing. Part of your skill to inspire lies in preparing your company and your audience to appreciate ambiguity over fixed and authoritative semiotic structures that *tell* you what can only be *imagined*.

But even when the theatre provokes strong feelings, in the long run, its repercussions are neither irreversible nor excessively painful, despite their instantaneous force. Onstage, violence, no matter how monstrous, is still a moment in dramatic time, which will end as soon as the lights go up in the house, and the audience leaves the auditorium. A poignant memory may be conjured up through a gripping soliloquy, an evocative visual environment, or an aural score. Yet, as audience members, we have been trained to accept that in most cases, what we are going through is nothing more than an *a priori* endorsement of a fiction, a "willing suspension of disbelief," to borrow British poet Samuel Coleridge's coined phrase. That said, the long-standing illusion that theatre is an altogether sheltered realm, a space that is not pressing for immediate answers, can be manipulated to directors' advantage. The fantasy of safety can allow for reflection and affect to creep into the experience of the moment while still supporting the comforts of ease and perspective. In the end, a sharp staging will always inculcate a sense of liminality and risk, even if it invites the audience to absorb things by proxy, gradually, and in layers. Despite coming in a rush, inspiration produces emotions and impressions that are by no means ephemeral.

> The filter of mediation offers perspective, a necessary solace in our confrontation with reality. The duality of *distance* and *identification* is inbred in the theatre experience, and, therefore, you can connect with your spectators also by manipulating their privilege to experience both.

Facilitating Experimentation

Unusual treatments of space, rhythm, movement, lighting, or character, introduced into the narrative frame, are reached for through daring experiments in the snug context of rehearsal. To energize the group and keep motivation alive, it helps to periodically reveal your own sources of inspiration. Using the collective "we" sets up the foundations for mutual exploration and reinforces the company's rapport. Sometimes, sharing stories—however personal or embarrassing—can offset a director's assumed entitlement and control with a condition of vulnerability, making it easier for the group to join the participatory journey of production as an equal voyager.

Given that theatre artists work collectively, they are bound to draw inspiration purely from sharing. Inevitably, they will recycle inside jokes, intriguing mistakes, and memories (e.g., a snapshot from a company tour or a really misbehaving spectator), only to unknowingly adjust them to the needs of each show. Since inspiration is contagious, such collective spirit is vital. To use a characteristic example from current theatre practice: at the beginning of a new project, Wooster Group's director, Liz LeCompte, is reported to ordinarily gather together her actors, designers, and technicians, and pay attention to their suggestions and what they may bring to the table, be it a book, a picture, a piece of music, or an item of clothing. She may invariably laugh or groan, in the meantime gathering useful performance material and creating the conditions for collective sharing, while they "stumble around inside their own heads in what could be called a first rehearsal" (Kramer 2007, 53). Animating things in rehearsal can also be achieved with a touch of lightness and a sense of play. Simple pedagogical strategies seem fully applicable here. As a rule of thumb, if you give performers a challenge—however big—adding an element of fun to it, they will do wonders. Many ensembles, including British company Complicité, use a variety of devising strategies based on impromptu exercises and physical drilling to train their conceptual imagination to generate physical metaphors. Complicité's director Simon McBurney insists that sitting around "banging tables and chairs for hours on end" can eventually lead actors to mini revelations, to coming up with a character "just kind of out of desperation" (qtd in Tushingham 1994, 17). Understanding directing as pure childlike fun and getting actors to just *play* with each other can expedite the group's physical and emotional partnership. In fact, a convivial atmosphere and a sense of festive occasion are fundamental to the bringing together of the environment, actors, and spectators. Espousing Lecoq's physical training, in which collaborative work is central, McBurney prepares his company's bodies and voices by toning the "muscle of the imagination" in search of a "moment of collective imagining" (qtd in Giannachi and Luckhurst 1999, 71). Similarly, UK-based Forced Entertainment's Tim Etchells likes to instigate an atmosphere of ease during the early stages, where "things find their own place" (qtd in Giannachi and Luckurst 1999, 25). He starts with developing materials that the company is "vaguely interested in, such as a couple of fragments of text, an idea about space, some ideas about costume or action or whatever," also recycling from an "old set or whatever is to hand" (25). In the same spirit, Collins invites the company to watch films and videos together: "we'll watch any kind of video we can get our hands on, because there's always going to be something interesting in it. It gives us something to collectively react to, something that exists in its own form already" (2016).

Such guilt-free work approaches seem particularly popular with practitioners who ordinarily work outside the restrictions of preexisting texts. Without the safe anchor of a fixed script, the emphasis is on establishing the right conditions for collective discoveries. Canadian theatre and film director and actor Robert Lepage improvises with both text and images, often to decide which works better as a way of developing the narrative. After trying out different objects, pieces of dialogue, or ideas, there comes a moment when everything will inevitably connect. "Suddenly," Lepage explains, a specific image "strongly conveys this thing I was trying to say. So you could cross off that dialogue because the images say it better. Other things are better said spoken; so this image is redundant" (qtd in Shevtsova and Innes 2009, 129). A permissive perspective takes pressure off of performers and sets up promising paths, drawing on the conviction that every fresh thought, lived moment, or *found* material can be dramatized. That, together with the understanding that inspiration lies within the grasp of the most heterogeneous sources—the Internet, interviews, documentary narratives, extracts from improvisational workshops, instructors' manuals, and old-time clichés, among others.

Inspiring is also a matter of facilitation. Or, in French director Ariane Mnouchkine's poetic description, a director is like a "midwife": "I help to give birth. The midwife doesn't create the baby. She doesn't create the woman, and she's not the husband. But still, if she's not there, the baby is in great danger and might not come out" (qtd in Delgado and Heritage 1996, 187). In the rehearsal room, which is the primary bedrock of all creativity, the group can work with free association to cultivate a context of research and improvisation with elements that are not necessarily restricted to the words of the play alone. Mnouchkine's long-established method of *Collective Creation* (Fr. Création Collective) has been an underlying compositional element of her dramaturgy. Soleil's company members research different historical, dramaturgical, and stylistic elements, basing their performances on material that has been accumulated during a thorough study of themes, characters, stories, or other provocations.

Overall, strategies for stimulating creativity are extremely diverse. For Katie Mitchell, visualization exercises provide ways of building "pictures of past events to support the action of the play" (Mitchell 2008, 90).

Others, like Declan Donnellan—also British-born—enter the text through singing and dance, and, more specifically, the tango (Giannachi and Luckhurst 1999, 19). Bogart, whose Viewpoints method of actor training has been applied in various educational as well as rehearsal contexts, trusts the "specificity of physical" work to render the performers more fluid onstage. Her intuitive approach has the actor embody character by responding to the text primarily through movement. She accesses the play kinetically as opposed to relying exclusively on psychological motivation because she is convinced that "by setting the form, the inner life is freed" (Herrington 2000, 159). On the other hand, Collins inspires his ensemble through challenge. He insists that he doesn't like to have a plan. "I would rather have just an assignment or a good and interesting problem to solve; a problem that would only be solved through work and rehearsal, that I wouldn't be able to sit down and write up the answer to" (2016).

These examples serve to ascertain that there are as many ways to communicate and inspire as there are directors working in the theatre. The ambition to create innovative experiences for spectators permeates directorial practice, from renowned "autocrats" from an earlier generation like Japan's Tadashi Suzuki or Wilson, who exactingly choreograph their actors down to the minutest gesture, to the organic, generous work of Peter Brook to the democratic delegation of tasks in companies that specialize in immersive and site-specific theatre. American auteur Peter Sellars hits the nail on the head when claiming that [what directors do in the theatre] "is just plant seeds [...]. What will be important will emerge much later" (qtd in Delgado and Heritage 1996, 235).

And a word of caution: throughout your work, it is crucial to remain anchored on that first reflex response that the text stirred in you. It is a commitment that can protect you from compromising an electric connection in favor of fancy, half-baked choices you might find easier to handle. It will also communicate the urgency of your interest to your actors, who can, in turn, inspire with their performances. Trusting the rhythm and the expanse of the collaborative venture can lead you to accept that eventually, by elimination and a discerning exploration of alternatives, you can discard most inessentials. Add to that the obvious fact that an in-depth, unhurried scrutiny of choices can only enrich the core of your work. Nevertheless, because the zeal to share your enthusiasm may sometimes get the better of you, the challenge becomes to let the zest sit. Give yourself time for some quiet reflection, which can only help you communicate your ideas in clearer terms and propose unequivocal challenges for actors and designers, your valuable co-interpreters. But that is the subject of the next chapter of the book.

WORKBOOK 1.2

Practice 1. Activating the Imagination

These exercises can be applied as warm-up activities at the beginning phases of rehearsal when the company is still getting to know the play. They function as a means of reenergizing the creative muscle of both director and actor.

Activity 1. Being Inspired

> Invite your actors to think of a favorite image, poem, or story; a recent memory; or an encounter which in some way or another inspired them.

> Ask them to identify the mood of the moment, its "emotional temperature." What colors would they use to paint this image/poem/story? What title would they give it? Would there be any characters in it? Any music?

Activity 2. Shaping into Form

As a follow-up to the previous exercise, actors can put into dramatic form a short, one-act play based on the original source of inspiration. Their job is to compose a piece with or without dialogue. For example, they can just decide on the movement and shape of the action, and write it down in detailed stage directions. Alternatively, they may also insert text, having first decided on matters of theme and style. Give them at least 15'–20' to develop their script, and then encourage them to have a rough go at staging it. Ask them to break into groups, and after some time of rehearsing, act their pieces out. Since they are working on their chosen material, they will most likely respond warmly to the exercise.

Activity 3. Working with Transformation

Have your actors think about different ways of transforming recognizable objects or sounds onstage, relying on poetic (directorial) license. They can, for example, improvise a scene from their play of choice, applying sets of staging patterns that suggest transformation. Feel free to add more patterns (images, objects, sounds, etc.) and expand on this list, according to the challenges you want to set up. Possible patterns may include:

- A plain wooden chair turning into a tree, a bookcase, a bed frame.
- A giant actor being miraculously dwarfed into childhood.
- A door suddenly opening to reveal something unexpected, such as a beach or a mountain ridge.
- An untraceable haunting sound emanating from an unlikely source, such as a woolen hat or a coffee cup.
- Three to five different ways a bed mattress can be used.
- Three to five different things a chair can stand for.
- Three to five different actions involving flowers.

At the end of the exercise, the actors can discuss their choices and review how particular patterns of staging added meaning or surprise to the scene. Encourage the group to also talk about the challenges of working from the "outside in," that is, starting from a specific form and finding their way back to the text.

Activity 4. Building on Inspirational Material

Actors will be asked to bring to rehearsal any material—a poem, a newspaper article, a favorite prop, a piece of music, etc.—that they consider relevant to the play or to their role. In particular, they should be prepared to discuss what aspects of their character this material reveals. The key here is not to let the censoring hand of embarrassment or reservation limit the potential for inspiration. You can circulate ideas to establish a practice of mutual, honest sharing. Despite the occasional surprise at the unlikely choice of material, in many cases, even the most "extreme" selections will soon start making sense and feel integral to the making of the play.

WORKS CITED

Benedetti, Robert L. *The Director at Work*. Englewood Cliffs: Prentice-Hall, 1985.

Bennett, Susan. *Theatre Audiences. A Theory of Production and Reception*. London and New York: Routledge, 1990.

Bogart, Anne. *A Director Prepares. Seven Essays on Art in Theatre*. London and New York: Routledge, 2001.

Cole, Suzan Letzler. *Directors in Rehearsal*. New York: Routledge, 1992.

Collins, John. *Interviewed by Avra Sidiropoulou*. New York, 2016 (unpublished).

Damasio, Antonio R. *Descartes' Error. Emotion, Reason and the Human Brain*. New York: Putnam, 1994.

Delgado, Maria M. and Paul Heritage, eds. *In Contact with the Gods?* Manchester and New York: Manchester University Press, 1996.

Giannachi, Gabriella and Mary Luckhurst, eds. *Directors on Directing*. London: Faber and Faber, 1999.

Herrington, Joan. "Directing with the Viewpoints." *Theatre Topics*, Vol. 10, No. 2 (2000): 155–168.

Ibsen, Henrik. *Little Eyolf*. Trans. D. Eldridge. London: Methuen Bloomsbury, 2011.

Kramer, Jane. "Experimental Journey." *The New Yorker*. 8 October 2007.

Lehman, Hans-Thies. *Postdramatic Theatre*. London: Routledge, 2006.

Mitchell, Katie. *The Director's Craft: A Handbook for the Theatre*. London and New York: Routledge, 2008.

Rich, Frank. "Auteur Directors Bring New Life to Theater." *New York Times*, 15 October 1985.

Roose-Evans, James. *Directing a Play*. New York: Theatre Arts Books, 1968.

Shevtsova, Maria and Christopher Innes. *Directors/Directing: Conversations on Theatre*. Cambridge: Cambridge University Press, 2009.

Shklovsky, Viktor. "Art as Technique," in *Russian Formalist Criticism. Four Essays*. Eds. Lee T. Lemon and Marion J. Reiss. Lincoln: University of Nebraska Press, 1965: 3–24.

Tushingham, David. *Live 1: Food for the Soul. A New Generation of British Theatre Makers*. London: Methuen, 1994.

Chapter 2

Interpretation

Imagination and Mediation

Interpretation is the result of a long process of sustained inspiration, a distilled awareness that comes from immersing deeply into a work of art or an intellectual enterprise. Epitomizing an aesthetic inclination and a philosophical outlook—what and how you essentially want the play to mean to your audience—it is an individual mind's unique product, after a stimulus has been mediated through mental examination. In this sense, it is both a condition and a result of consummate artistic creation.

Fostered by imagination—the "capacity to find and communicate imagery by analogy and metaphor"—(Black 1991, 25), directorial interpretation is communicated by a clear production *concept*, which develops from an original stroke of inspiration and culminates in the synthesis of different skills and sensibilities. It involves an understanding of life's complexities, an ability to analyze texts and grasp subtext, a consistent and robust style manifest in unified choices of staging, and a capacity to translate abstract notions into playable actions. Formed progressively from an initial response and connection to an idea, it is also a filter that allows the audience to become an attentive, sensitive recipient and a co-participant in the theatre event.

Besides being inspirational guides, directors are also instigators of interpretation for their company as well as for the audience. They lead by mobilizing an intricate, competitive, and visceral exchange, where the meaning (the essence, the message) of the work always remains fluid and is determined by factors that influence individual hierarchies of cognition and value. Indeed, according to the European Poststructuralist thinkers, every text is an open field of interaction between author and reader, where meaning is generated jointly. Back in the 1970s, Umberto Eco and Roland Barthes theorized on the distinction between "open" and "closed" as well as "readable" (French *lisible*) and "writerly" (French *scriptible*) texts, respectively. They both argued for the supremacy of texts exposed to multiple interpretations by multiple readers. Transferred to theatre practice, the idea that meaning is democratically created—being a shared property rather than the privilege of one single person—establishes an *a priori* understanding of the ensemble's as well as the audience's authoring involvement in the making of the performance.

The complex network of individual readings notwithstanding, directors hold the master key of interpretation. This involves responsibility and risk, as it releases your standpoint (together with that of the playwright) about fundamental issues of life and the self. Being, as British theatre and film artist Phyllida Lloyd suggests, the "link between one world and the other [...] like a medium, the director is there to unblock all the channels and to imagine how one world (the audience) might be perceiving the other (the production)" (Lloyd qtd in Giannachi and Luckhurst 1999, 55). Or, in the words of Peter Brook,

> When I hear a director speaking glibly of letting a play speak for itself, my suspicions are aroused, because this is the hardest job of all. If you just let a play speak, it may not make a sound. If what you want is for the play to be heard, then you must conjure its sound from it.
>
> (1996, 45)

The director functions as a (self-)empowered mediator between the writer and the audience, drawing on and unifying the individual readings of the company members, as they too grapple with the challenges of seeing a performance through—from inception to completion.

Some theatre history: at the beginning of the twentieth century, with the "Theatre of the Straight Line," the Russian pioneer director Vsevolod Meyerhold first described the relationship between author, director, actor, and spectator. Meyerhold postulated that the director—having absorbed the author's concept—conveys his ideas to the actor, and, in turn, the actor—having assimilated the author's vision via the director—stands face-to-face with the audience, supported by both the director and the author. Therefore, the actor freely reveals his soul to the audience, intensifying the fundamental theatrical relationship of performer and spectator (Meyerhold 1998, 51–52). In this way, Meyerhold argued, the audience is "made to comprehend the director through the prism of the actor's art [since] above all, drama is the art of the actor" (52–53).

```
>>> >>>> >>>> <<<<<
---x----------------x---------------x-----------------x---
```
Author Director Actor Spectator (50)

Keeping Meyerhold's schema in mind, we can also think of interpretation in terms of a complex journey along the horizontal and vertical axes of an imagined pyramid. The director balances evenly between those two pivots in a course governed by both stability (knowledge, imagination) and mobility (sharing, collaboration). Surrounding the pyramid is the "real world," an archetypically conceived universe, defined by laws ordinarily accepted as human, which are, however, adjusted from artist to artist, reader to reader, and society to society. This is theatre's essential matter. First experienced through the senses, the original grasp of the world is then subjected to intense brain activity and eventually becomes a story that bears a distinct formal identity.

Playwrights have held a prominent position at the top of the interpretative pyramid. Fundamentally, they isolate aspects of an amorphous material—impressions of life, significant historical facts, or observations about human relationships—and then work them into dramatic form.

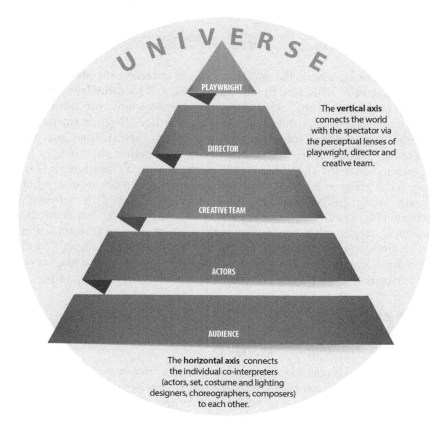

Figure 2.1 The Pyramid of Interpretation. ©Babis Melikidis

Creative intersections occur in the middle zone of the pyramid, the space occupied mostly by the director's mental operations and collaborative processes. In effect, directors are both creators and mediators. They will interpret the playwright's (preprocessed) perceptions and build an original creation, in tandem with the company's artistic contributions, which are meant to develop and refine their ideas further.

Directors are situated at a crucial intermediary station between the two termini of the interpretative spectrum: vertically placed between the "universe" and the "audience," and horizontally connecting and consolidating the creative collaborators' interpretations. Being by far the most flexible travelers, they move comfortably along the pyramid's two hinges during all stages of interpretation. Even if it appears to be the mental product of one, their reading is anything but unilateral, having been distilled from a variety of creative and critical perspectives, including those of the playwright, the performers, and the design team.

At the pyramid's base, the audience expects to receive the playwright's creation, already arbitrated by the *mise-en-scène*'s focusing lens. In perceiving performance through a chain of interpretations, spectators become its co-interpreters and, therefore, its co-authors. Their hermeneutic contributions, varying substantially according to their inclinations, are choices to follow, different threads that hold together the tapestry of receptions. It is for this reason that at the pyramid's bottom we can discover a great number of readings, intermittently contradictory but equally engaged. The exciting rendezvous or collision of the external, recognizable world, the world of the text and the inner world of the audience, suggests that any work of art can only grow in its interaction with a live component. Inevitably, the directors', actors', designers', and spectators' insights are much more than simple readings of a play; they are performative intuitions, embedded in the practice of authorship.

WORKBOOK 2.1

Practice 1. Working across Genres

The following exercise functions as an introduction to the world of the play and a way of reworking fundamental stories across different literary forms. It can be of use to both directors and actors.

Think of a central scene from your play of choice. Create a collage with visual images that place the events of that scene into an imaginary environment to which you feel especially connected.

Ask your actors to concentrate on the environment of a specific character.

Encourage them to write short poem, a short story, or a parody sketch that tells the character's story. This can be next rehearsal's homework.

Practice 2. Getting Started

How do you get started? What is the best way to introduce a new project to your company? To begin with, it helps to articulate your ideas with passion and clarity. It is also useful to give everyone a taste of your work methodology.

We are applying tasks and exercises on Tennessee Williams's old-time favorite, The Glass Menagerie (1944), which here serves as a possible model play, to illustrate the interpretation process.

Activity 1. Primary Considerations

Here is a list of considerations that you may want to take into account when you prepare for a new production.

The sociocultural context of the play as presented in the text.

Recurrent structural motifs that permeate Williams's *oeuvre* in general.

Recurrent themes across Williams's work (social exclusion, memory, illusion vs. reality, confinement, the importance of the past, the loneliness of the big city, frailty and violence, alcoholism, etc.).

Emblematic productions or adaptations of the play across different media; productions that may have established unique character representations.

Particular requirements of staging expressed in the playwright's production notes. The importance of stylistic devices such as the screen on which images and words from the text are projected.

The symbolic use of props.

The use of music.

Williams's detailed stage directions and the level of compliance to or divergence from them.

Activity 2. Conceptualizing

This simple technique is all about identifying and sharing your special connection to the play you are directing.

- Give a summary of the play, the context in which it was written, when it was first produced, and its critical reception. Reflect on why you think the play should be presented today.
- Share your private reasons for choosing to mount the play.

Example: "When I was a young child, I felt left out. I was never included in any school game and I was too shy to take part in group activities. During the break, I stayed in the classroom because I was too afraid to go out and look for a place to hide. I wasn't actively bullied, but I always sensed people watching and wondering what was wrong with me, and that made me feel even more excluded. Things got better when I grew up, but reading the play for the first time in college, I instantly identified with the character of Laura. When I started directing, I just knew I had to deal with those childhood issues. I'd like our audience to realize that we can all be cruel in so many different ways."

Activity 3. Thinking about Context

Here, you can elaborate on your reasons as well as the strategies of updating the play in a new spatial and temporal setting.

Example: "I would like to set the action in today's time, in a nondescript Western country. Laura is forced to leave school as a result of being bullied. The space seems permeated by the subterranean violence of a contemporary urban metropolis, anonymous and grey. The Wingfield's household is a faceless dark apartment in some nameless neighborhood of the city center. I will create an acoustic environment of TV sounds and muffled noises of the next-door neighbors seeping through the apartment walls. My idea is to suggest visually and aurally the alienation and lack of human contact that characterizes life in big cities today."

Activity 4. Scenographic Concept

Here is an idea of how a general concept about the setting can be discussed in more concrete stage terms. You may point out not only the functionality of the theatre space but also the way key scenes are structured scenographically and share dominant motifs, metaphors, or symbols that have influenced specific choices.

Example: "I see Laura's world more as a prison than as something tender and fragile. I believe that the set should emanate an acute sense of claustrophobia, as if the walls of the house were coming together to crush Laura with their force. The design will feature angled walls to reinforce the characters' asphyxiation. The fire escape stairs used by Tom is a significant scenographic element, which I intend to evoke through lighting, and stay committed to a principally abstract design. I am going to use very few furniture pieces—three chairs will do—and stage props. I am, however, interested in showcasing Laura's glass collection visually; my idea is to hang several pieces and sizes of crystal from different levels of the stage to create an attractive lighting effect."

Activity 5. Ideas about Costumes

Share with your actors your ideas about the costumes—will they be period, timeless, or contemporary? Since one of your goals is to create a unified mise-en-scène, the concepts of set and costume design are usually presented simultaneously, being chiefly interdependent.

Example: "The costumes will be timeless, nondescript, mostly in dark hues. They may, however, feature some retro elements that reference the original historical time of the play. A period hat for Tom or a shawl for Laura will do. I will, however, make a display of Amanda's fancy prom dresses, all in an array of bright colors, in order to underline the contrast between her dazzling past in the South and the present-day dreariness of her life. A couple of them might even be hanging from the ceiling by a fishnet."

Activity 6. Ideas about Sound

Because music is an art to which most can relate, talking about it in rehearsal is bound to stir up passion and interest. One idea would be to invite your actors to contribute to the discussion with musical choices of their liking, which might in some way be associated with the play or their character. They may, for example, think about their character's favorite song and play different options in rehearsal.

Example: "The world of the play harbors an undercurrent violence, which I would like to express musically. The performance will feature atmospheric jazz melodies and a mix of dissonant percussion sounds that, put together, can synthesize an urban soundscape. I hear sounds of faraway sirens, drunken mutterings of passers-by, and snippets from neighbor chats in various languages. I intend to also make full use of the musical motifs that Williams indicates in his stage directions—they are solid clues for approaching the character of Laura and the emotional atmosphere of the play as a whole."

Activity 7. A Rough Rehearsal Plan

In the first rehearsal, while the new project is introduced to the company, the director doesn't have to get into too much detail about the work with the actors—this is something that, after all, requires a degree of trust and can happen gradually. Explaining your rehearsal plan is nonetheless useful, especially if you are thinking of employing innovative techniques or a fresh methodology.

Example: "We have two months of rehearsal before load-in. We will dedicate approximately two weeks to table work, looking at themes and imagery, bringing in research, and applying Stanislavski's system of scene analysis as well as settling actions and objectives. Then, we will get on our feet to improvise basic themes of the play (such as loneliness, rejection, need to escape). Soon after that, we will start blocking the play and also revise objectives and actions, accordingly. I am hoping that we will be in a position to have our first run-through within five weeks from now."

"Ethics": Playwrights, Directors, Auteurs

Whether acknowledged as primary or secondary agents of textual meaning, directors, playwrights, and actors have often competed for control of interpretation. In fact, the question of the director's role as "author" (in French film theory, *auteur*) of the performance remains pressing, even as the practice of ensemble creation has emerged stronger in the new millennium. Already in the 1930s, Antonin Artaud vehemently argued for a radically reconceptualized style of directing. Further supported by the establishment of "directors' theatre" in the 1970s and 1980s, the understanding that a director is much more than a mere translator of the dramatist's text has rendered the boundaries and the so-called "ethics" of interpretation fluid and slippery.

For the most part, directors are still considered equal, and on occasion, even more pivotal composers of the theatrical script. Their authorial prerogatives are based on the premise that every performance is a text in itself, written in a language that is a fusion of discursive and sensory discourses and in a vocabulary that is nonetheless unique to each artist. With that in mind, the idea that any director is capable of fully realizing the author's intentions needs to be reframed. A new staging is also an original text, invariably determined by the force of imagination, particular life conditions, needs, and ambitions, which both control and free up different assumptions and patterns of association. In practice, this suggests that you can engage actively with the imagery, memories, and ideas that the words on the page stimulate, without obsessing about the existence of one "correct," author-friendly interpretation. In many ways, you can serve the text and the playwright better, even if in some cases this service won't be blatantly apparent. American playwright Richard Nelson discusses the unique parameters of the writer-director collaboration as

> [The] beginning of the courtship from the playwright's point-of-view, when the director makes that jump of confidence and then becomes the protector of the play in that regard…I don't expect when the director sees the world of the play he'll get it all right away, every moment of it; otherwise, why do the play? It's more that a director should feel that the world of the play will be a pleasurable world to be in and to explore. That he senses the world and wants to be in it, as opposed to changing it.
>
> (in Nelson and Jones 1995, 63)

Throughout the twentieth and the twenty-first centuries, some playwrights have resented directorial liberties and launched significant assaults—occasionally with unwarranted harshness—against naughty transgressors of texts. British dramatist Arnold Wesker's attack on directors and on what he termed a "führer complex" back in 1988, is telling:

> A madness is sweeping through European theatre, perhaps through world theatre. It is a madness which has elevated the role of the director above the role of the writer. The stage has become shrill with the sounds of the director's vanity; it has become cluttered with his tricks and his visual effects. No play is safe from his often hysterical manipulations.
>
> (Wesker 1988, 63)

In the same vein, much more recently, another celebrated British playwright, David Hare, caused an uproar amongst fans of nonmainstream theatre. He pointed a finger to European *auteurs* for "all that directorial stuff that we've managed to keep over on the continent" and which is now "coming over and beginning to infect our theatre" (Hare in Sweet 2017, 69).

One can only think of acclaimed experimentalists such as Thomas Ostermeier, Mitchell, or Ivo van Hove, who have tirelessly recalibrated the appositeness of canonical texts. Working mostly with the classics, these directors will update the dramaturgical or stylistic frame of the plays, without, however, compromising their themes and powerful impact. Thankfully, in the broader community of contemporary theatre artists and audiences in the West, measuring the efficacy of interpretation against the degree of fidelity to the playwright is no longer as necessary or as popular as Wesker and Hare would have us believe. Such polarizing calibration would, after all, condemn the function of the director to that of a stage illustrator of words as opposed to an interpreter. To cover the multiple aspects of this controversial debate is well beyond the scope of the book. Suffice it to say that because the relationship and collaboration between directors and playwrights have to date remained fraught with tension, any critique of the practice of interpretation would benefit more from precluding assumptions of how meaning is hierarchically produced. It is worth focusing instead on the ways theatre-making works—how ideas are impregnated, born and communicated, their departures, adventures, and arrivals. In our attempt to avoid patronizing terms like "loyalty" or "respect" to the dramatic text, we could argue that the pyramid of interpretation is defined by the director's instinctual and profound rapport with the playwright's work. The particular channels through which the textual *Weltanschauung* is perceived and expanded also affect interpretation.

Given that the complex relationship between writers and directors will, in the end, determine the production's shape, the act of interpretation has been repeatedly and awkwardly regarded as an attempt to strike a balance between the playwright's assumed "intentions" and their translation onstage. However, the very word "intention" is subjected to various degrees of misunderstanding and abuse. It could be more useful to view directorial interpretation as a reflex and extraction of what a text means to a director, rather than an obligation to render "objectively" something as abstract and treacherous as an intention.

In the context of collaborative engagement, the individual impressions of actors and designers will be adjusted, in varying degrees of compliance, to the director's overall vision of the play. And unless the operational principle of the company is that of a collective, the *condition sine qua non* is that during the delicate stages of conceptualization, all the involved artists will more or less operate from within the structure set up by the leader of the group.[1] In the majority of theatre projects, while actors are responsible for interpreting character, directors exercise artistic control and are held accountable for the entirety of the production; they draw from their colleagues' creative work but remain orchestrators of the interpretation. And while complying to the director's authority does not, evidently, apply to ensembles that build performances collectively (see, e.g., UK-based Faulty Optic or tangledfeet, both of which exploit more communal principles of theatre-making), in some experimental theatre groups that still claim to function as ensembles, decisions will eventually gravitate toward one person assuming responsibility for the production's comprehensive form. In those cases, the artist-leader or artistic director is distinctly designated and ordinarily determines its signature style. Among notable examples are Théâtre du Soleil's Mnouchkine, Complicité's McBurney, Elevator Repair Service's Collins, The Builders Associations' Marianne Weems, or Gheko's Amit Lahav. Emma Rice, of the British theatre company Knee-high, defies the function of a theatre collective in an observation that testifies to the director's authority: "There can actually be a real freedom in someone saying: 'I am going to make the decisions.' You need that in the rehearsal room. I often find myself saying 'Strong but wrong' when someone makes a suggestion" (qtd in Gardner 2004).

All that said, in the day-to-day practicalities of each project, the title of "arch-interpreter" may be of little operative significance. In many productions, in the absence of a given dramatist, the director—or often the ensemble—will assume primary authorial function. In fact, the offshoot of the ongoing battle between playwrights and directors—each side claiming authorship as well as authority—has been the proliferation of models of performance where a preexisting dramatic text or a single artistic agency is no longer the be-all and end-all. These include physical and devised theatre, dance, site-specific and immersive theatre, and numerous types of mixed-media adaptations and intermedial/multimodal structures, including Internet, cyborg, android, and robot theatre. In (and by) these new categories, the notion of textuality is continuously reviewed and expanded, with several discourses and aesthetic tropes being critically interrogated during the preparation and rehearsal stages. In the work of many international companies in Europe and the United States—among which are DV8, Forced Entertainment, Frantic Assembly, Gob Squad, Kneehigh, and others—which showcase innovative performance forms, the functions of writer, director, and performer often coincide, and the text, if at all present, is de-dramatized and treated more as material for formal exploration and less as subject matter *per se*. There will be more to say on this later in the book, when we address the subject of alternative dramaturgies.

WORKBOOK 2.2

Practice 1. The Play in our World

This exercise can help you determine some aspects of the text that seem central to your interpretation. We are using Sophocles' Antigone, a play about familial honor and personal integrity as the play of choice.

Consider how Sophocles' tragedy relates to our world today. Think of what might have inspired the playwright to write it, and decide if there is some particular outlook with which you, as director, particularly identify.

- Think how this perspective fits the reality around you and make it as immediate and relevant as possible. You may, for example, wish to examine a social or moral attitude or political viewpoint, as is the idea that those in power can be prone to implacable rigidity. Think about Creon's inability to bend his authority to embrace the familial law.
- Is there a phrase in the text that you find particularly engaging? If there is, make sure you share it with all your collaborators.
- If you are confident about your chief interest in the play, you should now envisage ways to express it with consistence in your staging.

Practice 2. Shaping a Line of Interpretation

This exercise is good for building rapport and developing a common vocabulary with your design team, which is a necessary step for formulating a common aesthetic approach to the production. The following is another example from Sophocles' Antigone.

Set a first production meeting with your designers, where ideas and feedback on the play can be exchanged. This is your chance to clarify your concept and invite your team to contribute to it.

- Ask the set designer to create an image—a sketch, a model, a rough idea of the set—taking special note of the sense of decadence and moral sickness in the play. Throw in your thoughts. Would, for example, a cluttered space be more appropriate for evoking the disintegration of human values in the play? Would a clinically sleek set or an empty stage better capture a world where feelings of compassion have been replaced by the thirst for power?

- Ask the composer to come up with a soundscape that resonates this primary line of interpretation. What instruments would best convey it? Would you use music, sound, or silence to impress Antigone's resistance to King Creon's tyrannical attitude? If there were one single natural sound that could be used in performance, what would this be?

- After meeting with the designers, have targeted rehearsal with your actors. Invite the actor embodying Creon to think of three different physical ways to portray the character's obdurate stance. They may be in the form of still images, but the posture and gesture should be as detailed as possible. You can continue this line of work for the other characters of the play.

Practice 3. In Your Own Words

The following activity is meant to give your actors distance from their role, so that they can begin to grasp the play as a whole. It can also be useful for enabling directors to make conscious choices about what needs to be told, what is significant in the play and should be communicated more emphatically.

Have your actors to take turns summarizing the play of choice and then share your own version. Summaries are constructive, in that they tend to reveal economically your connection to the text and serve as a basis for company members to build on. The way you enter the story and the elements you consider worth including or else eliminating suggest an investment to specific ideas and themes, that is, a preliminary directorial approach.

Practice 4. Do It Another Way

This exercise, proposing nontraditional, more intuitive ways of responding to text helps actors experiment with different modes of expression.

Identify the climactic scene in your play of choice. Ask your actors to read it out loud. When they are finished reading, give them time to think of ways to:

- Turn it into a song and sing it.

- Make it into a picture and draw it.

- Conceive of a sustained movement and physicalize it.

- Decide on a specific setting for it and describe it.

Finally, ask them to cast the play, having male actors perform female parts and vice versa and read out the scene once more, in this new configuration.

Point of View

Point of view (also, perspective) is the spine of interpretation, a compelling idea, the angle that signifies what the director perceives the text's constitutive meaning to be, a mental door through which an audience is initiated into the dramatic landscape. Delivered gradually, a strong point of view ideally conveys the presence of the text in the here and now. When it features an inner rationale and is handled imaginatively, it can remarkably influence the production's sensory, affective, and critical outcome.

Protagonists vs. Antagonists

Conceptually, point of view hinges onto two different interpretative spindles: (a) the director's philosophical and ideological attitude regarding the text, and (b) the director's focus on a theme or idea, usually highlighted by a particular character. In the latter case, point of view is embodied in the character that best allows the audience to access the director's involvement in the story of the play.

Who is the protagonist?

Which character or idea moves the action of the play forward? Around which character or idea does the play revolve?

With which hero/antihero is the audience bound to identify?

With which hero/antihero or idea does the director identify?

Usually, the very title of the play is a strong indicator of point of view. Let us use another example from Ibsen, examining the fascinating love triangle story of *The Lady from the Sea* (1888). Ellida Wangel, who has been married to a placid country doctor, finds herself yearning for the ocean of her native village, increasingly drawn back to the memory of her old lover, a seaman who went missing, after making a solemn pledge that one day he would return to claim her. She waits silently for him, forced to live a life of convention, deprived of real freedom or self-definition.

In this play, the title instantly establishes the mysterious Ellida as the protagonist, whose inner turmoil seems to set the action forth. A woman at odds with her current marital, geographical, and sociocultural environment, Ellida is also unquestionably singled out as the play's heroine already in the title, following the title protagonist pattern of Ibsen's masterpieces, *Nora, Hedda Gabler, Peer Gynt,* and *John Gabriel Borkman.* Furthermore, the title unabashedly hints at fundamental archetypes (a Lady, the Sea), which are bound to influence narrative focus. It is small wonder that most directorial approaches will place Ellida at the tip of Ibsen's triangle, spotlighting her as a principal character carrying the story through to its conclusion. Several readers will instantly latch onto her dilemma, the conflict between reality and dreams, the choice between an earthy, perhaps ordinary, husband and a ghostly but intrepid lover. The possibility of a life of independence, which is so aptly embodied in Ellida, is probably the aspect of the text that most audiences would find attractive and worth exploring. Not surprisingly, it is Ellida's emotions and her strife to reclaim a sense of self, on which productions of the play tend to focus.

In examining how point of view is construed, it helps to consider if the "assigned protagonist" actually changes, and if so, exactly how the playwright advances this change over the course of the play. Reviewing emotional movement can help maintain a consistent narrative arc. For both directors and actors, tracing the line that runs from point A to point Z along the length of the character's life is therefore imperative, particularly if we hold point of view to be also a reflection of a state of indeterminacy, a capturing of fleeting impressions before the play moves to the (dis)comforts of closure. To further illustrate the point: it has often been debated that in Sophocles' *Antigone* (442 BCE), the real protagonist is not the celebrated title heroine, but her opponent, King Creon. The argument holds that the tragedy's shift in dramatic emphasis, on the one hand, concerns the ruler's changed attitude toward the unbending mercilessness of law and, on the other, endorses more forcefully his function as the catalyst that pushes the events to their tragic conclusion. Prompted by a similar rationale, Shakespeare's Iago has sometimes been made the envoy of directorial point of view, the designation—by ways of title—of protagonist status to Othello being consciously ignored.

Alluring as it may appear at first, an unorthodox point of view can flounder across the several stages of working on character and story. In Ibsen's case, depending on the nature of your connection to the play you may decide to spotlight Ellida's husband, Wangel—or, for that matter, her lover, Stranger—as your principal character. If so, you would be staging the production from his perspective and illustrating how his presence is instrumental to the way the plot unfolds. Such decision, however, is bold, and a perilous one, at that. The hypothetical premise that the audience will be captivated by Dr. Wangel's relatively unexamined private plight does not make a strong case for granting him protagonist status and may in fact hit against the play's structure. In the end, it is Ellida's decision that speeds the play to its resolution and her state of mind that gives it its thematic nucleus. Taking protagonist status lightly is therefore a risk you may wish to rethink. Examine potential complications carefully before adopting a heretical approach. While your interpretative standpoint is meant to shake up entrenched preconceptions and clichéd assumptions about the text, it helps to follow narrative development beat-by-beat before you endorse irrevocably brazen choices. For all their startling impact early on, radical alternatives have to be supported through the entire length of the show, to articulate, rather than iron out inherent textual complexities.

> In any radical choice you make, you need to consider whether your point of view might cause an irreparable imbalance to how you handle situation and structure, the subterranean tensions in the text and the particular aspects of character relationships.

Narrative Focus

Settling on protagonist status goes hand in hand with more practical point of view strategies, such as the decision, for reasons of focus, to bring a character/performer to the foreground on both literal and figurative levels. We will discuss the director's control of the stage and the way emphasis is applied through composition in another chapter. As far as the dynamics of characterization go, typical strategies of achieving focus include the following:

> Actors can be allotted a specific position onstage (center stage, fully lit) for stronger emphasis.

> Actors can be absent or semi-present (dimly lit) to introduce a quality of danger into the scene and so obtain a different kind of "outsider's" focus.

> Directors can associate every significant beat of a scene with a spe-
> cific character's presence—whether that presence is manifested phys-
> ically, or is merely suggested.

Time and again, you may wish to retain a point of view of neutral-
ity and deliberately stall the audience's emotional identification with
a specific character. Visual composition can deepen characterization,
defying conventional psychological analysis. Handled efficiently, stage
focus produces narrative impartiality, repudiating hierarchical designa-
tions of character. To that purpose, blocking—placing or moving actors in distinct physical positions and arrangements—can prove a most
effective strategy, impressing changing character dynamics between
scenes. For example, equal physical emphasis on more than one single
character, if not on all of them, suggests multiple narrative angles and
may underline unexpected tensions in the play. Similarly, to occupy
matching dynamic positions onstage, actors can be spotlighted simultaneously, be situated alongside a straight line or placed alternately at
each of the three tips of a triangle formed onstage. Different points of
view can also alternate visibly from scene to scene, just as narrative
voices interchange, one with the other. Last but not least, introducing a
narrator onstage, a popular Brechtian technique usually brings with it
a level of objectivity. The fact that narrators traditionally stand in for
the playwright's voice no doubt makes their presence strategic. To the
extent that they manipulate the audience's gaze, they seem to reinforce
authorial authority. However, they also allow for spectators' responses
to the text develop more democratically. In the end, a "neutral" treatment of narrative focus might serve a potentially unbiased approach to
the text, transcending an otherwise one-sided reading informed exclusively by your protagonist's perspective. There will be more discussion
of composition and blocking in the following chapters.

WORKBOOK 2.3

Practice I: Changing the Angle of Storytelling

*The following exercises usually take place in later stages of rehearsals when
actors are more familiar with the text. They can introduce your point of
view to the company, revealing subtleties of interpretation. In addition to
reinforcing the bond among the members of the group, as they collaboratively not only interpret, direct, and act but also become spectators for each
other, they suggest different ways in which perspective can be maneuvered.*

Activity 1. Switch the Element

Using your play of choice, ask your group to come up with two different stage versions of the same scene, keeping the text intact but changing one element in each of the versions (setting/character addition/doubling of characters, etc.).

Activity 2. Add to the Mix

Using your play of choice, assign to your actors a scene that you consider especially intriguing.

Define the elements as: (a) space/setting, (b) physical life, and (c) rhythm/pacing. Let the group experiment with these elements, and raise the level of excitement by introducing new parameters (bringing in another silent character; adding a song; adding a frozen tableau right before the scene opens, etc.). Ask the actors to describe the scene's principal event and then present a brief version of the scene (with or without words).

Ask the audience (the other actors) to comment on the different ways the story was told, and determine the dramatic event in each version. Were different aspects of the story revealed, every time the perspective changed? Did they obtain new insights into the world of the play? Were the characters portrayed in a different light?

Practice 2. Who Is the Protagonist?

This exercise helps settle point of view and build consistency in the storytelling.

In your play of choice, focus on a scene that features at least two characters.

Ask your actors to consider two or three possible ways of staging same scene. In each of those, place a different character at the center of the action. Have the actors think of ways to make the audience "follow the scene" through this character.

Ask the audience (the other actors) to observe how the story unfolds in each of the different versions. Were they able to perceive which character held the key to the story? How did the overall atmosphere of the scene change from one version to the next?

After these questions have been addressed, ask your actors to describe the way they worked to approach the scene.

- If they kept dialogue and setting intact in all different versions, how did they handle emphasis?

- Did they change the blocking, and if yes, how did that affect the scene's dynamic?

- Did they experiment with the posture and gestural life of each actor in a way that illustrated which character "owned" the story?

Practice 3. Making Narrative Choices

Letting the subconscious do most of the work, this exercise is suitable for both directors and actors. Once you decide what is essential for you in the text, you will be more confident about the relevance of your connection. Your actors can also identify better with the character they are impersonating, coming up with clues, details, and ways of accessing the role that might have otherwise been overlooked.

Carefully reread your play of choice, and give an account
of the story to an audience as an omniscient, third-
person narrator. Then, retell the story in the first person,
identifying with one particular character in the play. To
whose character's story are you mostly attracted?

Now, try to retell the story from a different character's
perspective, still using the first-person singular. Do
you notice any considerable digression as far as the
description of the plot or the emotional texture of the
dramatic situation goes? If yes, explain why this is
the case.

Ask your audience to make a mental note of any
particular moment in which your account of the story
deviates from the original play. These are precisely the
points that will help build your directorial point of view.

Practice 4. In Character

*An improvisational exercise, this is also a no-strings-attached attempt
at free writing. It helps you consider character aspects that you may
have ignored and also gives actors a sense of closure and a more personal take on their role. The exercise can be followed by "hot-seating,"
a popular rehearsal technique, where each member of the group gets to
ask the seated character questions about the life of the character, the
choices made, motivations behind specific actions, etc. The following is
an example from Ibsen's The Lady from the Sea.*

Have your actors read the play and examine the character of Ellida
closely. They should write, and then take turns reading out loud
or performing, an interior monologue in which the title heroine
addresses her audience and justifies her final decision to stay married to Wangel.

Practice 5. Titling

"Titling" urges you to consider the essence of the play and experiment with interpretative angles.

> Select a segment from your play of choice, pivotal to what you consider the play to be about.

> Give it the first title that comes to mind.

> Give it a journalistic headline.

> Give it an emotional—first-person-singular—title.

> Give it a pseudo-objective third-person-singular title.

> Notice if these titles converge toward a common line of interpretation.

Metaphor

Point of view can be further validated by the application of fitting metaphors of space and setting, action, situation, and character. In its most common usage, a metaphor is a literary phenomenon in which a verbal element such as a word or a phrase, meaning one thing, represents an idea or an action in a way that is not literally true, but suggests a resemblance. In other words, something is applied figuratively. For example, a ring can be a metaphor for marriage, a person would "kill for a drink," and a "darkness growing inside" metaphorically points to a state of grief or even suicidal thoughts. In the world of directing, a metaphor is another term for *concept*, the primary stage analogy, conceit, or choice that communicates your vision and gives consistency and coherence on the levels of structure, language, and design. To a large extent, the use of the proper metaphor contextualizes themes and ideas and also refines style and stage semiosis. A contemporary military camp can aptly depict Macduff's army forces in Shakespeare's *Macbeth*; a sea-front quay of a small Mediterranean island might be the right backdrop for Aeschylus' *Suppliant Women*; a rave party could host the Walpurgis Night scene in Goethe's *Faust: Part I*, which brings to life a debauching congregation of witch spirits.

Albeit primarily literature-based phenomena, metaphors are also constitutional principles of visual narratives, driving the symbolic function of set, costumes, and props. Because sounds and pictures are more easily "recognized transnationally than (unfamiliar) languages," pictorial and multimodal metaphors allow for "greater cross-cultural access than verbal ones," stimulating a more immediate emotional appeal (Forceville in Gibbs 2008, 463). Resonant metaphors support interpretation in patterns that communicate meaning in a timeless but also timely manner. Conceived early on during the director's preparation phase, they can be later engineered into concrete forms, which can either felicitously confirm or put a spin on the play's historic, culture-specific identity. Now and again, a metaphor will coincide with a familiar symbol, a concrete element that expresses an abstract idea or emotion. Symbols are powerful stage signs, by which the audience accesses the elements of staging more directly. They are usually highly evocative in communicating prevailing moods and textures. Overused symbols—aka clichés—such as roses referencing love and sexual passion, white costuming to foreground innocence, blue lighting for the depiction of nighttime, red lighting for blood and violence, and so on, are frequently exploited for their ironic or parodic effect.

Some directors are exceptionally good with metaphors. In German artist Thomas Ostermeier's *Nora* (2006), a bold reading of Ibsen's *A Doll's House*, the body of Torvald (Nora's husband) collapses into a huge fish tank at the center of the set, after he was literally attacked by a magazine that Nora fired at him. On a revolving stage, acclaimed set designer and Ostermeier's lifelong collaborator, Jan Pappelbaum, created one of his usual hyper-naturalistic open-plan spaces that transferred Ibsen's late nineteenth century drama into the living room of a European middle-class family of today. Rather than rely on the trite visual expedient of a golden cage, Ostermeier used the fish tank as a disturbing symbol of marital imprisonment. Similarly, in Ostermeier's *Hamlet* (2011), the metaphorical use of scenography once again pushed the textual limits: Elsinore was depicted as an expanse of graveyard, littered with beer cans—the mess and mud onstage reflecting the play's obsession with death and decay. As Ostermeier explained, "There are so many reasons why the dirt and the earth make sense... It's a playground, it's a cemetery, Old Hamlet's grave" (qtd in Dickson 2011). Insanity, loss, and rage were physicalized in the metaphor of the set, the endless graveyard upon which the actors enacted their miseries, rolling into dirt and even swallowing it.

> Set is something bigger than the environment in which the action takes place. The physical world of the play is a metaphor for its theme. For example, a crowded space of heavy furniture pieces for Vanya's bedroom/estate office in Chekhov's *Uncle Vanya* is meant to intensify the sense of claustrophobia that he experiences in his uneventful provincial life.

> Costumes are metaphoric of the characters, bearing visual clues that reveal different qualities of status, background, and personality. A conspicuously tight corset can therefore act as a symbol of female oppression.

> Lighting can be a metaphor for action. It differs from set and costumes in that it relates to time, as well as to the three-dimensional space. Shadows communicate the atmosphere of danger; a slow cross fade of a soft warm wash can introduce dawn, and a new day in the action.

In equal measure, the most compelling and viable metaphors tend to feel both contemporary (relevant to current concerns) *and* timeless (signifying archetypical patterns of human motivation and behavior). In a rereading of Euripides, Katie Mitchell's 2011 *Women of Troy* conjured up the ghost of the ravaged city by envisioning an industrial cityscape near a modern-day port. Confined to a timeless iron prison, female inmates in fashionable gowns vented off their despair while occasionally dancing to familiar tunes or smoking cigarettes, as the world around them was falling apart. Mitchell's careful selection of metaphors supported the tragedy's weight, holding off the allure of sensational but ultimately portentous updating.

In light of this, watch out for the enemy of literalness that resides in overly ambitious metaphors. The danger is that in your attempt to either stretch or bend the original text to fit your concept you may end up with a reductive visual or contextual statement. Classical plays featuring a military setting—be they Euripides' War Plays or Shakespeare's Histories—often fall prey to heavy-handed metaphorization. Sometimes, the action is haphazardly relocated to any culturally fraught site that would seemingly provide a modern audience with instant references (e.g., the extensive metaphoric presence onstage of contemporary refugee camps and battlefields in the Middle East or the Balkans). Along similar lines, imagery directly pointing to an overtly corporate context—most notably, the Stock Exchange's trading floor—has been standard metaphoric fare in plays featuring a street-wise "market" discourse. In themselves, these choices harbor no performance disasters. Many directors, however, relax in, if not entirely rely on, simplistic correspondences of text and context, refusing to challenge them against complexities that can only reveal themselves gradually. Without being further developed, metaphors may impose superfluous adjustments to the directorial approach, overlooking the risks of arbitrary updating.

In your use of metaphors

- Fight the urge to succumb to the instant gratification of "right-on" symbols. Realize that metaphors should serve rather than smother the embedded circumstances of the text.
- Think through the allure of a sweeping image that you expect will instantaneously recontextualize the play.
- Test your metaphors against the givens of the play and the dramatic arc and see how they help the story unfold naturally, through time.
- Search for subtle alternatives; although perceptually taxing, suggestive staging makes for a far more rewarding audience experience than feeding on obvious metaphors.

Settling on a metaphor is an exciting and delicate business, and, ideally, the factor of clarity will outlast the momentary hype of straightforward analogies. Resonant metaphors are dynamic. Their viability will eventually be tested by the actors, who are responsible for bringing them to life, and by the performance itself, particularly with respect to the functions of space and dramatic time.

WORKBOOK 2.4

Practice I. Visualizing

This exercise brings your understanding of the play into your everyday life. Establishing a coherent ruling metaphor is the first step toward making your concept appear less contrived to an audience. The following is a personal reading of Miller's Death of a Salesman.

- Think of an emotionally charged scene from your play of
choice. Decide on the main dramatic event, the one situation that defines structure and content and without which
the scene appears meaningless to you. Let your imagination loose and rethink the scene in terms of your immediate circumstances. Think of any physical places and social
settings that come to mind. Think also of what is happening in the world around you. Is there anything in your
present-day reality that you see represented in the play?
If yes, what is the connection between the "now" of your
world and the "then" of the text?

Example: "In *Death of a Salesman*, the scene in Howard's office is
pivotal to the play's theme, namely the idea that people have become
commodities to be disposed at will. In this scene, Willy initially asks
Howard, the director of the company for which he has been working
nearly all his life, to be transferred to the New York office, tired of being
on the road for several years. In the end, after begging and arguing his
case in vain, he ends up getting fired, since he has grown old and is
therefore of no further use to the company. The scene evokes distressing
images of life in several contemporary metropolises afflicted by a sustained financial crisis. Middle-aged people are made redundant, as the
job market plummets, and households go bankrupt. The suicide rate
is rising fast, while many sleep in the streets. Willy's desperate plea to
Howard gives flesh and blood to this contemporary metaphor":

-Howard, all I need to set my table is fifty dollars a week.

(62)

[...]
-If I had forty dollars a week –that's all I need. Forty dollars,
Howard.

(64)

- Try to conceive of one single image, which, put onstage,
would direct your audience's attention to the point where
reality meets the playwright's words. Is this image an element of the set, a costume, a projected visual, or video?

Example: "The portrait of an elderly man in an oversized suit and
shabby shoes, battered briefcase in hand and head down, speaks
volumes. He aimlessly roams the streets of the Downtown area
of a big city—could be New York, London, or Athens—against a
crowd of people walking past him and paying no attention to the
fact that he is talking to himself."

Practice 2. Working with Clichés

You can exploit stage clichés (lighting filters, extremely fast or slow movement, set elements such as water, overly ornate costumes, a huge gilded crown to indicate power, or a suitcase to suggest an imminent departure) to your advantage, extracting their universal value and using them for emphasis and irony. The following exercise explores the dangers of literalness and compels you to rethink overused symbols in unpredictable ways.

In your play of choice, think of any cliché that could successfully represent the main idea you wish to communicate about it. Concerning setting, look at emblematic spaces, such as hospitals, schools, mental wards, prisons, and courtrooms. Also explore "cliché-props," such as flowers, weapons, technological equipment, phones, and so forth.

- How literal or subtle are your metaphors? What do they reveal about the principal events of the play?
- Do your setting and object metaphors provide a clear reading of the play?
- Would you consider using different metaphors for different communities of audiences?

Of Taste and Style

The notions of directorial taste and style are deep-seated in the act of interpretation. Taste can be defined as a preference or specific aesthetic inclination, whereas style is the manner in which this preference ends up defining a work of art, be it something written, built, designed, or performed. Because of their function as conceptual properties that carry an artist's signature, both style and taste reference a particular artistic disposition. And, while taste is natural and inbred, style is something that can be cultivated. At the same time, because they are *mediums* and not *products* of imagination, taste and style should not to be confused with *form*, which suggests a manifest product of style. In effect, style is the idea that drives an aesthetic choice, whereas form reflects the way such choices are aligned in performance. Style, as we will soon see, can be developed by means of research, which brings forth elements intrinsic to the playwright's period, including the cultural mores and staging conventions of the time.

Irrespective of the particular style you are working in (contemporary, historical/period, or timeless), paying close attention to the original circumstances of the play helps render them applicable to the concerns of a modern audience. After all, whichever the production style, it must feature an inner logic and combine all elements of staging consistently. If, for example, you decide to stage Brecht's *Mother Courage* (1939)—a play set during the Thirty Years' War across Europe (1618–1648)—in ahistorical, timeless style, you would obviously leave out any seventeenth century references and avoid full period costuming. The evolution of style is also vastly influenced by how a director exploits textual analysis, performance venues, and casting. To tackle the brutal urgency of short rehearsal periods, it helps to be fully aware of the intended style and also have some solid suggestions to share on how you plan to achieve your goals within the given time and budget limitations. In ideal conditions of extensive rehearsal periods, you can modify your original concept together with the actors and the rest of the company. Even then, however, preparation is essential for your style to drive an effective production plan.

> Style runs through the director's intuitions, giving distinct identity to the production form, and synchronizing the energy of the original play with that of the present-day world. You can build style first by researching different historical contexts and then, using this research, by formalizing an innate artistic intelligence, which can be further triggered by the text and perfected by the diverse possibilities of the stage.

Collaborative teamwork notwithstanding, the production should in the end feature a unified, and, ideally, also original style. That can be a documented reliance on technology (see, e.g., the Wooster Group or the Elevator Repair Service); formalist choreography (Robert Wilson); a raw, industrial look in the set design (van Hove); imagistic composition (Bogart); or a proclivity toward hyper-naturalistic detail (Ostermeier). In general, most directors' work is usually characterized by a particular and recurrent style, a preference for specific techniques and combinations of elements that mark production choices. And, although style is not necessarily an "acquired taste," it is typically developed by constant exposure to different stimuli, experiences, and work methodologies. Discovering and polishing your style is therefore part of a lifelong education, which gets more and more specialized as you become better versed in forms that feel necessary, that is, relevant to express (interpret) at this particular moment in time.

WORKBOOK 2.5

Practice 1. Defining Your Style

In spite of the general nature of this exercise, there is value in labels and (self-)definitions: they point to recurrent patterns in methodology and support a more informed awareness of style. Becoming more conscious of the principal areas of strength or weakness in your work can lead you to sound adjustments and bolder choices.

Consider your predominant directorial style. Use Shakespeare's *Macbeth* as a basis for virtually exploring your favorite patterns.

- Are there any recurrent aesthetic motifs in your work?

Would you use an eclectic set or costumes to reflect the tragedy's timeless subject matter? Would you incorporate surrealist elements in the scenes of the witches? Would you apply symbolic overtones for the final battle scenes?

- Are there any rudiments of staging you tend to favor?

Would you use live music onstage for the battle scenes? Backlighting for the murder scenes? Projections of the different locations in the play?

- Do you like to work with big sets or are you a minimalist?

Would you consider staging *Macbeth* on an empty stage, relying on evocative props to add texture to your *mise-en-scène*?

- Do you layer your productions with dance and song? Will you add period details?
- Is stylized movement a must in your work?

Would you stage the coronation scene as a pantomime?

- Do you object to period costumes?
- Are you mostly a conceptualist, a minimalist, or a fan of Realism who works well with detail?
- Do you tend to work with physical and visual forms or are you primarily drawn to dramatic theatre?
- Are you a "faithful director" or a modern-day adapter?

Would cutting down the play to an hour-and-a half piece with three to eight characters ever be an option?

Practice 2. Styling through Art

This exercise is a chance to experiment with different styles, periods, and forms, and bring a painterly perspective into performance. It can be quite useful for building mood and atmosphere.

Select a work by three different painters from distinct periods and styles. Concentrate on a particular scene in your play of choice. Plunge into the atmosphere of the artworks and build three different versions of the same unit of a scene, inspired by the style of each of the paintings. As a fun model exercise, you can look at some paintings that have been praised for their exceptional composition, such as those by Rembrandt (The Anatomy Lesson of Dr. Nicolaes Tulp [1632] or the Nightwatch [1642]); Diego Velasquez (Las Meninas [1656]); Marc Chagall (I and the Village [1911]); or Pablo Picasso (Guernica [1937]). The following is an attempt to describe the impressions drawn from American artist Edward Hopper's famous painting Nighthawks (1942). The work was said to represent an existing diner in Greenwich Village in New York City, close to where Hopper lived. According to Hopper, it depicts the isolation of a big city.

- Briefly describe the setting and the figures in the painting:

Example: "The painting depicts a nighttime diner with a counter, metal tanks at the back, and four characters in different relationships to each other. A couple (man-woman), a barman, and a male figure with his back turned to the viewer seem to be the only patrons of the restaurant."

-   Build a story that takes into account: (a) the time of the day, (b) the setting, and (c) the characters' physical actions and their inner life.

Example: "It is night-time. The story takes place in an American-style diner. An attractive young woman is eating a sandwich, and a shrewd-looking man next to her is presumably engaged in conversation with the waiter. There is another man with his back to us, adding an element of unease and possible threat. The characters are sitting close to each other, but there seems to be no physical contact between them. However, the couple shares a secret. They are lovers, involved in an illicit affair, that the man considers ending."

- Reflect on the atmosphere the painting emanates.

Example: "What is especially appealing to the painting is its enigmatic atmosphere. The darkness of the outside, with the red brick houses and the empty road, mirrors a state of introspection and quiet reflection, even though, traditionally, diners are places that bustle with life."

Practice 3. Which Style for Which Play?

The following is a versatile activity that could be used in the early stages of rehearsals. It familiarizes you with different styles and helps you experiment with a variety of approaches.

Make a simple list of the periods or styles that you consider appropriate for staging a particular script. For the sake of experimentation, work alternately within a naturalistic/surrealist/symbolist framework, and introduce different stylistic approaches. For example, you could use Magic Realism, with its jarring intrusion of the unexpected and the fantastical into a predominantly realistic narrative frame; alternatively, a stark documentary concept or a postapocalyptic style with a bare stage, harsh lighting, and an ambient soundscape. Decide which style best serves your vision of the play.

Note

1 It needs to be pointed out that in recent scholarship, the notion of the ensemble is by no means limited to a group of actors working together but embraces the entire scope of making theatre. According to Radosavljević, the ensemble way of working seems to "represent a work ethos which is collective, creative and collaborative—whether by means of individual members making the same kind of contribution (devising) or making distinct kinds of contribution towards the same artistic outcome (writing, directing, composing, designing, performing)" (2013, 11–12).

WORKS CITED

Black, George. *Contemporary Stage Directing*. Fort Worth: Holt, Rinehart and Winston, Inc., 1991.

Brook, Peter. 1968. *The Empty Space*. New York: Touchstone, 1996.

Gardner, Lynn. "We like Our Plays to Be Foolish." 19 July 2004. Web. 24 October 2016. http://www.theguardian.com/stage/2004/jul/19/theatre.

Giannachi, Gabriella and Mary Luckhurst, eds. *On Directing*. London: Faber and Faber, 1999.

Gibbs, Raymond W., ed. *The Cambridge Handbook of Metaphor and Thought*. Cambridge: Cambridge University Press, 2008.

Meyerhold, Vsevolod. *Meyerhold on Theatre*. 1978. Trans. Edward Braun. London and New York: Methuen Bloomsbury, 1998.

Nelson, Richard and David Jones. *Making Plays. The Writer-Director Relationship in the Theatre Today*. Ed. Colin Chambers. London and Boston: Faber and Faber, 1995.

Sweet, Jeffrey. *What Playwrights Talk about When They Talk about Writing*. New Haven and London: Yale University Press, 2017.

Wesker, Arnold. "Interpretation: To Impose or Explain." *Performing Arts Journal*, Vol. 11, No. 2 (1988): 62–76.

Chapter 3

Method, Leadership, Collaboration[1]

Preparation

Directing is both an art and a craft. It feeds on imagination, intuition, and openness, and relies on discipline, problem-solving and focus. What the word "method" suggests is nothing more and nothing less than the balance, in different degrees and proportions, of various talents and skills. Resolving issues of blocking, efficiently handling entrances and exits, observing sightlines, facilitating the physicalization and delivery of text, monitoring beginnings and shaping endings of scenes, can all be said to belong to directorial technique. Grasping and foreseeing strengths and weaknesses in acting, design, physical and rhythmical patterns, narrative development, point of view, and dramatic intensity is more a matter of intuition and artistic intelligence. Knowing how to speak to the team, communicating with passion and firm resolve, motivating, encouraging, and adjusting one's strategies when addressing different people with different issues, are gifts that seem ingrained into someone's personality. However familiar these observations might be to the experienced director, it may be worth reiterating how the different stages of the practice engage different faculties and aptitudes.

Especially for those new to the art, it is useful to lay out some of the rudiments of directorial routine that have to do with the director's preparation, a phase which runs through the entire production and permeates all aspects of collaboration. After all, at the beginning stages of any project, before you even enter the rehearsal room, you are expected to have frequent conversations with the producer and the design team, to discuss your ideas. Later on, in rehearsal, your preparation will navigate the team through the anxieties borne by the novelty of each situation. And while you are not expected to have all the answers, clear objectives formed by solid preparation will make it easier to confront challenges that include but, alas, are by no means limited to a cast of performers that have so far been strangers to each other, a highly poetic text, a complicated set, or an unconventional rehearsal method. To know is to be in control, and showing up prepared can safeguard a degree of directorial authority within the company.

Researching the World of the Play

Preparation starts as soon as an idea for a specific project forms, long before rehearsals begin. Whether it is working with the playwright or a dramaturg to resolve structural and stylistic issues in the play, collecting material relevant to the original period or the production's context, or meeting with the designers individually, the director needs to have done his or her homework. As early as you embark on a new undertaking, it is practical to create a production promptbook, in which to include all your research and notes to the actors and yourself. A director's diary—or "the bible"—the promptbook is where you document rehearsal progress, add fresh ideas, mark entrances and exits, insert changes in blocking, and incorporate lighting and sound cues, together with suggestions to actors. A good promptbook contains at the very least the script and a ground plan of the stage, but entering updated information and observations about the play is an extra bonus.

Research (textual, visual, auditory) is a big part of the preparation stage and crucial for understanding the play's foundations. It can address a number of factors, many of which naturally fall into the domain of textual analysis and will be discussed in more detail in the following chapters:

- Historical and social context
- The playwright's dramatic/nondramatic *oeuvre*, in general
- Relevant facts about the time in which the play was written
- Relevant facts about the time in which the play is set
- Critical reception
- Influences as well as impact
- Production history
- Prominent thematic and structural motifs and patterns.

Research develops out of the information—direct or indirect—that the text gives you. In Anton Chekhov's *Uncle Vanya* (1896), for example, you get enough clues about the play's social context when Astrov discusses with Sonya the life of the peasants (Act II). Similarly, you are exposed to emergent ideas in the writer's time, as when, once again, Astrov shares his ecological vision with Yelena (Act III). References to the dire conditions of the Russian farmers, which the playwright had empirically experienced himself, are ample. Moreover, the text comments on the ineffectuality of the Russian intelligentsia to implement necessary changes. Additional research into Chekhov's nineteenth-century Russia will further reveal how this vast empire mostly relied on agricultural economy, boasting of no industrial production. Wealth was accumulated on the upper classes, whereas the lower classes were impoverished. One can also read the play through Chekhov's prism at the time he was writing, growing fatally sick, and reflecting back on opportunities missed.

Your research homework can cover things like consulting secondary sources, reading other works by the dramatist, together with plays and nondramatic texts of the same period and related literary movements. Visual research, on the other hand, may include paintings, photographs, films, or video footage from the playwright's period, directly or indirectly referencing the text. Your research on Ibsen's plays, for instance, could include works by the Norwegian expressionist artist Edvard Munch, and most notably those explicitly indebted to the playwright, such as the oil painting *The Lady from the Sea* (1896), which was quite obviously inspired by Ibsen's title play. Studying different theatrical conventions and identifying stylistic elements related to the historical period of interest may also help you gauge the immediacy of the effect that the play had on its original audience and suggest metaphors suitable for updating it.

Research makes the play personal to directors, actors, and designers, given that "a piece of architecture may suggest a world; a painting might hold the key to the way a character moves; a piece of music could inspire the structure of a dialogue." In fact, it does more than provide information. It "sharpens perceptions of art and of the world" and "shows the director forms that express the feelings dormant in the text" (Black 1991, 102). But while archival research on the play and its context is necessary, a different kind of impulse-based preparation is also valuable: your first emotional responses, which usually concern striking elements in the script, may strongly influence your concept of staging. Go to rehearsal with ideas, memories, images, and even trivia, closely or loosely associated with the text, and share them with your company.

We have already covered how originality resides in imagination. Using your emotional responses to build the world of the play is a way of envisioning the stage as an independent lived space, rather than the domain of (theatrical) artifice. Constitutive qualities that point to setting, period, and social attitudes are conveyed associatively so that your actors and designers will have an opportunity to respond intuitively to stimuli that are not entirely text-based. In turn, you can formally shape such uncensored responses by setting up rules that lead to concrete choices and make sense in the context of your production. Every staging introduces its own formulas *vis-à-vis* the way time operates, how people dress and speak, what is considered polite or rude, what some gestures denote, and so forth. Lists of factual or invented information are helpful in adding unusual detail to an environment devised from scratch. It follows that research normally occupies a broad and stimulating part of the director's preparation stage, and can be considered "the director's paint palette. The less research done, the fewer colours will be available" (Baldwin 2003, 23).

Production Choices

For a period spanning from a few weeks to a few months before rehearsals begin, directors will meet regularly with producers and the design team to make key executive decisions. Basic prerehearsal choices include venue, casting, building, or hiring a company and deciding on a concrete role for the audience. These decisions are customarily reached in agreement with the producer.

The following issues must be considered carefully:

- Whether auditions will be required for casting, and how many actors need to be hired.
- Where and when the auditions will take place.
- Whether the company is already formed or whether additional collaborators will be involved.
- Rehearsal space and rehearsal dates—the number of rehearsals needed.
- When and where the set design will be constructed.
- When the set design is due to be delivered.
- Whether the set design is portable, in case the production transfers to a different venue, or tours.
- Any special technical requirements; equipment that will be used for rehearsals and performances (e.g., video projectors, the rental of [additional] lighting instruments).
- Any special seating arrangements that must be fixed immediately, if they are to affect the production design (e.g., the audience will be standing/moving/sitting on the floor).

Casting

Not every director is trained or intuitively competent enough to hire the best actors, and yet imaginative casting is one of the highest determinants of a successful run. In fact, according to Tyrone Guthrie, it is 80 percent of a play's interpretation, while another British director, Richard Eyre, also quotes a very high percentage number:

> sixty to seventy per cent, not just in type and the suitability of an actor's looks and ability for a particular role, but also that you feel you

will have a relationship with the actors and that they will fit into some kind of social group. Part of the business of directing is to engage a group of people and engender a happy and homogeneous entity.

(Qtd in Cook 1989, 29–30)

In reality, casting is an inbuilt element of point of view. In its most enterprising forms—including cross-gender; cross-racial; and even more adventurous, *post-human* choices, such as the use of cyborgs or androids onstage in robot theatre—it undermines existing assumptions and highlights less prominent aspects of the story and character portrayal. Notable examples of unusual casting include Fiona Shaw performing the title character in Deborah Warner's National Theatre's production of *Richard II* (1995) and Glenda Jackson performing Lear in Warner's *King Lear* at the Old Vic (2016). Also, Kate Valk's doubly fascinating blackface embodiment of the archetypical tyrant Brutus Jones in the Wooster Group's celebrated production of Eugene O'Neill's *Emperor Jones* in 1992. On a different note, one should surely take note of Oriza Hirata's casting a robot in his 2014 version of Frantz Kafka's *Metamorphosis*.

In auditions, directors evaluate how an actor's particular skills and personality attributes will serve a specific role but also the general requirements of the production. Acting skill notwithstanding, the ability to take direction is a major casting consideration. In a focused audition, you should try to detect how actors respond to challenge and discomfort. That being said, and given that not every actor is good at auditioning, watching someone perform in an actual live theatre environment is still the best preparation for casting successfully. All in all, auditioning skills come with experience. Young directors can only benefit from being exposed to different audition processes. Practice, for example, will teach you how to recognize an actor's level of talent and skill beyond a deceptively perfect performance in the audition. In the same manner, you will learn to foresee the unique talents that an actor can bring to the process and decide whether these fit the overall concept of the *mise-enscène*. On the other hand, as troublesome as it sounds, you should also be able to predict potential difficulties in a future collaboration. Here too, intuition is vital. The way questions are framed, how notes are given, the type of improvisations, the physical exercises, and actions the actors engage in during the audition—it may be a particular song or an elaborate dance movement—must be attuned to the nature and requirements of the project for which you are casting.

Venue

Theatre spaces have their secrets, which they unfold gradually. As with casting, a level of experience, combined with spatial awareness and a basic knowledge of marketing, can lead to attractive choices of venue. Why pick a proscenium stage? What kind of mental associations does a particular space emanate? Is there a special community that surrounds the theatre building? Does the theatre have its own audience? Does it rely on subscriptions? Is it a publicly sponsored or a private theatre, and how does that affect the practicalities of rehearsal time, ticket sales, and promotion?

Team Building

Choosing your team members on a stroke of powerful impulse, discerning judgment, or calculated risk can be a mark of wisdom and experience. Acting on your intuition alone during casting is, however, never enough for building your company of artists. Concentrate on the reasons why specific artists are suitable for specific projects, without underestimating the significance of luck and random circumstance, which can lead to sound or, reversely, detrimental casting choices in auditions. Do the actors' training backgrounds match, and if not, is that a problem? Are the performers likely to complement each other and eventually develop into an ensemble? Can you foresee any conflict of personalities, and would that be a serious consideration?

Determining a Role for the Audience

Whether actively integrated into the performance or not, the nature— if not the degree—of the spectators' engagement is also considered at the onset of the project. Just as the director-producer team may take into account the age; gender; ethnicity; and the social, economic, and linguistic background of the audience, it is equally important to have a sense of what may be expected from the spectator before and during the performance. In the case of site-specific or immersive work, such considerations have probably already infused writing and composition. Nonetheless, even when the production assigns more conventional roles to the audience, it still needs to be decided where this audience will be seated, if there is going to be any active interaction with the stage or whether the spectators will be asked to move to different places or seats during the show. Similarly, it must be determined if there is a change in the location of the audience between scenes or if the actors are going to approach spectators at some point of the play, and with what intention. Such concerns are not exclusively practical; they establish concrete perceptual frames and are inseparable from the production concept.

Flemish director Ivo van Hove is an expert at making theatre space resonate with visceral complexities, and can literally rebuild playhouses to adapt to his scenographic vision. For the New York Theatre

Workshop production of Ingmar Bergman's *Scenes from a Marriage* (2014), together with his ingenious set designer Jan Versweyveld, he created three separate "mini theatres" for the first half of the play. The audience had already been divided into three groups. Each group was invited to become a witness to Marianne and Johan's (performed by three different sets of actors) marital adventures, following them through each of the three spaces and occasionally eavesdropping on what was going on in the adjacent rooms, from which it was but subtly divided. In the second half of the show, the world of the characters/ performers and the world of the spectators merged into one big empty space, all erected walls having been brought down during the 30-minute intermission. The spectators of the three groups were ultimately brought together, surrounding the actors on all sides of the bare black box, submerged in the domestic drama that was being enacted for, against and around them.

WORKBOOK 3.1

Practice 1. Make Your Promptbook

The following checklist could keep you organized in your daily directing routine and help you prioritize essential reference material in rehearsal.

Decide on the things that you would like to include in your promptbook. Choose among the following elements:

- Your research: information about the playwright, production history, visual research, and period information.
- Calendar and rehearsal schedule.
- Contact sheet for company members.
- Your notes: by scene/character.
- Your ideas: whenever a new thought strikes you as useful, you can mark it down for future reference.
- Your blocking directions: they can include diagrams of actors' positions and movements from scene to scene.
- Notes and suggestions for actors.

Practice 2. The World of the Play

Addressing the following questions can give you a macroscopic view of the play and its main thematic, structural, and aesthetic motifs. You can also perceive the world surrounding the text more synthetically, which can lead to a higher stylistic consistency in the staging.

Read the final scene of Chekhov's *Uncle Vanya* (Act IV) and address the following questions:

- What kind of world do the characters inhabit?

  Uncle Vanya is a play about confinement and helplessness. It focuses on people's difficulty to escape from their limiting environment but also from themselves. It is a dreary, claustrophobic world, with little hope for change.

- What is the main dramatic event (situation)?

  The final act of the play is the epitome of resignation, providing glimpses of a disheartening future for Vanya and his niece Sonya, in which nothing much can be changed.

- What is the main conflict?

  In the play's final scene, the major conflict of Vanya against his life of stagnation comes to a moment of crisis.

- What comes before?

  A series of departures (that of Yelena and her husband, the old Professor Serebryakov, and a little later, of the idealistic doctor Astrov) gives the entire act its melancholy tone. The scene in question opens with Vanya and Sonya resuming their bookkeeping activities in Vanya's bedroom-office.

- What comes after?

  There is little indication that things will improve from hereon. On the contrary, the final scene suggests that the future for Vanya and Sonya can only recapitulate the past; uncle and niece will continue to live a life of mundane, practical work, locked in the family estate in the provinces.

- How is the physical life defined? Is it static? Dynamic? Is it a mixture of both?

  Following up to the vigor of the previous scene, where people bustled around in preparation for Yelena's and Serebryakov's departure, this is a remarkably static scene, underlining the sense of paralyzing boredom that is in the heart of the play.

- How private or public is the scene? Who is listening, and who is not?

  Contrary to the previous scenes, where everybody seems preoccupied by Yelena's and Serebryakov's departure, this is a quiet, private scene, a mutual acknowledgment by Vanya and Sonya of what their life is going to be like from now on. The fact that it takes place in Vanya's bedroom/ estate office, a sanctuary of sorts, reinforces the confessional and private mood. Apart from Vanya and Sonya, the other three characters present in the room get on with their routine activities silently, as if they have blended into the scenery. Telyeghin plays softly on his guitar, Maria Vassilievna takes notes, while Marina gets on with her knitting.

- Is there any sense of risk or danger? If yes, where is it coming from?

    There is no danger as such but a growing sense of dreariness for the loss of opportunities and the inevitability of a life of habit. Vanya painfully comes to terms with the fact that he cannot change his life circumstances and the choices he had made early on.

- What is the energy and the rhythm? Does it change over the course of the action?

    The rhythm is slow, melancholy, contemplative. Sonya's closing tirade, which ends with "Poor, poor Uncle Vania, you're crying! [Weeping] You've had no joy in your life, but wait, Uncle Vania, wait...We shall rest... We shall rest...We shall rest" (1959, 245) is meant as a consolation, and seemingly interrupts the gloomy tone with forward-looking energy. Nevertheless, its desperate repetitiousness and Christian undertones undermine the intended purpose to encourage Vanya to get on with his work.

- How does space change from one scene to the next?

    There is no change in the setting. The entire Act IV takes place in Vanya's bedroom-office. The only change introduced in the final scene of the play is that all external action has stopped; everyone is gone, and we can now experience the claustrophobia of Vanya's world in all its paralyzing stillness.

Practice 3. Visceral Response

This activity proposes an affective approach as you are encouraged to trust your senses and memories to help you free up any associations with regards to the text. Try not to stop yourself from sharing the very first thing that comes to mind. Avoid second-guessing or mellowing down the force and energy of your original response.

Select a play written and set in a period of time different from yours. Address the following challenges without resorting to the actual words of the text or envisaging any specific staging. Just try to imagine the everyday reality of the characters, the kind of place they live in and the actual things they do on a daily basis.

- When I think about [play] I *see* [three different images]
- When I think about [play] I *hear* [three different sounds]
- When I think about [play] I *smell* [three different smells]
- When I think about [play] I *remember* [three different memories]

Consider, also:

- The season: whether it is wintertime, spring, summer, etc.
- The time of the day and whether a passage of time is indicated.
- The landscape (urban, rural, island, desert, etc.).

Practice 4. Draft Your Rehearsal Plan

What follows is just one version of a "rehearsal map" to keep you on track. You can make a point of revisiting it at the end of each week (or each rehearsal) to check if at least some of the rehearsal goals have been met. You can also keep revising it if new or unforeseen circumstances come into play.

With the help of your Production Manager and Assistant Director, work meticulously, to plan out a two-month rehearsal period. Think of a viable outline for a six-day, six-hour rehearsal week, and mark the following rehearsal landmarks:

- Introduction of the project; introduction of the company; presenting the design concept/model (if ready); and discussing the overall production style
- First read-through
- Table work, scene analysis, character analysis, actions, and objectives
- Actors off-book
- Improvisations
- Blocking of scenes

- Revising the overall shape
- Experimenting with movement and props (if applicable)
- First "stumble-through"
- Making adjustments to blocking
- Run-throughs
- Working with detail
- Bringing in friends as a preview audience
- Moving to tech week

Practice 5. Check the Pulse of the House

This is another checklist, useful for gauging the progress made in rehearsals and identifying weaknesses and aspects in both staging and acting that need to be improved. It is especially applicable in a run-through.

As a director, you must attempt the impossible: shake off your insider's knowledge and perception of the work and watch the run-through as a first-time audience member. Take mental (rather than actual) notes, and focus on the overall impressions, emotions, and the sensory impact that the performance produces in you rather than limiting your attention to the details of blocking and the mise-en-scène. Trying to remain objective may be quite taxing, but if there is one moment to face up to your director's fears, this will be it. In fact, the exercise can brace you up against some real audience's reactions on opening night.

Watch one of the final run-throughs of the play, before moving to technical rehearsals. Try to be an "innocent spectator," and ignore the details of staging in what you see. Instead, let yourself be carried away by the energy and feeling of the performance as if you are watching for the first time. Have your objectives been met? Take mental notes of the following:

- Have your original ideas turned into meaningful imagery?
- Can we follow the narrative through visual storytelling only?
- Are the themes coming across forcefully?
- Is the story clear enough?
- Does the performance sag at any point? Does it keep you engaged?
- Are the transitions between scenes efficient and smooth?

Practice 6. *Listen Carefully*

If you pay attention to what is said and how it is said, you will be able to guide your actors to speak with a fuller awareness of what it is they are trying to communicate.

Ask your actors to run through a scene they have been recently working on.

- Turn your back to the stage and listen, as if you are hearing the dialogue for the first time. What are the main things that strike you in the story?
- Can you recognize the prevailing mood only by the rhythm of the piece and the tone of the actors' voices?
- Pay attention to the pacing, the emphasis paid on specific parts, and the overall energy.
- Are there any stakes? Does a particular action raise them at any moment in the scene and how?
- Is the dramatic situation clear enough? Are you missing anything? Intensity? Detail? A sense of connectedness among the different characters?
- Are the silences and pauses making sense within the scene's general rhythmic shape?

You can also record the scene and play it back to your company. You and your actors can then share feedback on what you have just heard.

- How well do the delivery, diction, rhythm, and emotional texture of the dialogue (and of any monologues) convey the story?
- Can you identify any shifts in emphasis or emotive levels?

Practice 7. *Entrances and Exits*

This exercise is about moderating the energy levels of the entrances and exits. It can be used to sharpen the actors' awareness of the stakes in each scene, organically bridging past actions with the circumstances at present, and with what is about to follow, without, however, forcing a sense of closure.

Have your actors improvise with different types of entrances and exits for different scenes of the play.

According to the mood of the scene, ask them to enter laughing, crying, absent-mindedly, in rage, or in some physical discomfort. Determine whether these choices serve your concept, and modify them, where necessary, also adding more detail.

Encourage your actors to reflect on what preceded the scene they are coming into, and express this energy physically.

Practice 8: Audition Checklist

A director's audition toolkit, this list of considerations is by no means exhaustive. Feel free to revise and expand it, as different combinations of requirements, targets, and hurdles are always bound to crop up.

Stage 1. Preparation

Have the actors been given enough time to prepare for the upcoming audition?

Have you specified clearly what the actors should prepare for the audition (a classical or contemporary monologue? a scene from a play? a song?)

Are the actors required to have read the play before auditioning?

Would you like the actors to bring along their resume and headshot?

Have you secured a comfortable audition space with all the necessary equipment? This might include a long table with chairs for the director, the casting director (if there is one), and the assistant director; a chair for the actor; a CD player or an iPod (if needed); a piano (if auditions are for a musical), etc.

Is there a lobby area for actors to wait for their turn to audition? Is there water (and perhaps some light food) for everyone?

Have you provided *sides* (excerpts from the script that actors will be reading as part of their audition) to everyone waiting?

Stage 2. The Actual Audition

Try to make your actors feel comfortable as soon as they come into the audition room. Engage briefly in light conversation, and invite them to talk about their interest in the project. You may ask them to introduce themselves in some unusual way (e.g., by using one telling gesture or posture, or a favorite phrase from a play).

In turn, introduce yourself and whoever else is present at the audition with you.

Record the auditions on camera, so that you can go back and review them at your own pace.

Take notes generously throughout the audition. Focus on what is important to you. You can also create your personal checklist form, in which to tick out the boxes or provide grades or percentages for all auditioning actors. You may, for example, include the following queries about the performers:

- Do they look the part?

- Do they fit your concept of the play (and the part)?

- Do they bring anything extra to the part?

- Can you hear them correctly? How good are they with speaking?

- Can you see them properly? How present are they physically?

- Are they interesting to watch? Do they attract your attention and keep it sustained at all times?

- Can they take direction? Are they more or less able to process fast enough the suggestions or adjustments you have requested of them?

- Can they handle surprises? (This can help determine how fast they will be able to respond if something unexpected happens in performance).

Make sure you keep the time so that the audition does not run behind schedule. Feel free to cut actors off (politely, but firmly) when they go past their allocated time.

Ask the actors who audition to give a different spin to their piece. Have them deliver their monologue to one particular member of the audience, do the monologue sitting, with their eyes closed, singing it, and so on. Do not be too persistent if you realize that the actor is having trouble making a specific adjustment.

After they are finished with their audition piece, have the actors ask you questions, and be prepared to gauge their intelligence and level of commitment to their art, in general, and the project, in particular.

When the time is up, thank the actors gracefully and give them an estimate of when you will be getting back to them with news.

Stage 3. After the Audition

Carefully review your notes, watch the videos of the audition sessions and make a short list (three to four people for each part).

Give time for the audition impressions to sink in. Allow yourself to be surprised by the discoveries made and by the fact that your ideas about a specific character have been changed or enriched by a particular actor's audition.

Arrange for *callbacks*, inviting your short-list candidates to further auditions. Those should ideally be targeted toward the play you will be directing. Have different actors engage in dialogue scenes and decide if they are a good fit for each other—whether they have good chemistry or their personalities seem to clash. More importantly, watch for any possible signs of lack of team spirit: do they tend to steal attention? Are they antagonistic toward their colleagues? Do you sense potential difficulties in a future collaboration?

Give it a few days and then call everyone back, letting them know if they have been cast in the play or not.

In Rehearsal: Leadership and Team Spirit

Directing is an art that balances out different sets of antinomies: control and sensitivity, discipline and encouragement, structure and experimentation, management of temporary tensions but also appeasement of severe conflict within the group. Your involvement and passion are vital for keeping the company interested and feeding the expectation that everybody's work will support a common vision. Mentally working in ideal circumstances, you are nonetheless expected to handle the demands of actual rehearsal with pragmatism. Because rehearsals are a private affair, ordinarily held sacred by all team members, most of what happens in the room will remain forever hidden from the public eye. Directors are "both inside and outside the experience of the play," they are reflectors "of the actors' impulses and the audience's responses, and yet always something else, something allowing [them] a view from 'elsewhere'" (Cole 1992, 64). As a surrogate audience, you are trained to anticipate the pulse of the house before the performance begins, and convey your insights to the company, making inspired choices. These, as we have already discussed, typically include the handling of casting, venue, blocking, and movement, rhythm and design, all of them being fundamental aspects of staging.

For the most part, accomplished directors possess any of the following personality features:

- They are *sensitive*: they can gauge the actors' strengths and weaknesses in rehearsal and performance.
- They are *flexible*: they adapt and adjust to the unique challenges of each project and process.
- They are *patient*: they are prepared to wait to see results.
- They are *disciplined* and *firm*: they know how and when to set boundaries.
- They are *collaborative*: they understand that the basis of creativity is shared ownership and participation. They have authority without being authoritarian.
- They are *resourceful*: they can come up with creative solutions, stepping in when things are at a standstill.
- They are *confident* and *secure*: they speak with conviction yet also take responsibility for their mistakes.
- They are *reliable*: they are always available for further feedback and dialogue, when appropriate.
- They are organized, economical, and practically minded.
- They are fully *present* and *alert* to everything that is going on in rehearsal.

All for Strategy

Before setting up a realistic, step-by-step plan for each project, most directors have already imagined, even if peripherally, the totality of performance. That often happens by "calculating restraints, challenges, and opportunities along the way, and calibrating and then recalibrating and designing and redesigning their strategic approach as the game evolves" (Genovese 2015, 20). And where the actor sees only the trees, the director is able to "envision the whole wood" (Roose-Evans 1968, 18) and make the necessary adjustments. As rehearsals progress, you will be fine-tuning different aspects of the concept—acting and design-wise—and building onto something that will soon start to resemble an actual performance. However, clear rehearsal targets should always be presented at the beginning of each session in the form of both practical and artistic notes and suggestions. They can either focus on something as specific as getting a special entrance to work or mark out a broader mission, as is improving the pacing of a sequence. Whatever the task, specificity is your most reliable ally, since ideas are best expressed in concrete images, and directions best put across in lucid, "actor-friendly" language. Too much intellectualizing and abstract language, rather than reveal your erudition and intelligence, will probably alienate actors, who are invariably trained in an action-centered discourse. It is crucial, therefore, that you monitor and harness, every step of the way, your tendency to fall into general talk.

In the best-case scenario, you will have already prepared a schedule detailing the timeline, from first rehearsal up until opening night. Even so, reality rarely meets the ideal, and next day's meeting times are sometimes only decided on the spot. However, most performers appreciate the security structure provides, and so planning individual rehearsals and run-throughs should take into account, as much as possible, different combinations of needs—practical and other. You can keep things on track with the help of an SM (Stage Manager) and an AD (Assistant Director), who are responsible for drafting the rehearsal schedule and making sure that people's time is spent efficiently.

For all intents and purposes, as a director, you will primarily *oversee* the process rather than impose on it. Interestingly, different systems of leadership in Management (such as "autocratic," "laissez-faire," or "shared") (Cooper 2008, 4–5) could easily apply to the reality of rehearsals, encapsulating various aspects of directorial methodology. After all, directors have invariably been labeled as "dictators," "gurus," or "coaches." Needless to say, each style has its advantages and disadvantages. While autocratic directors may function better at times of crisis and are perhaps suitable for supporting an inexperienced company, "actors' directors" are more inclined to give their performers initiative, an approach favored by mature and confident ensembles. According to the particulars of each project, a mixture of styles is also common. Whichever the case, it always works to lend an ear to your actors—their concerns are often question marks that can lead to significant discoveries.

In general, however, directors learn to respect the company's need to bond, without interfering much. Part of the challenge is to put together an involved group and not merely a sum of talented individuals. Once the bond becomes tighter, you may have little choice but to step aside and let team synergy develop effortlessly. The dilemma whether to control or delegate often presents itself in the beginning stages of the directors' careers when their rehearsal personality is not yet fully developed. That the notion of leadership has come to be identified with despotic behavior is erroneously based partly on the misconceived perception of the director as an insensitive ruler unwilling to listen or empathize. For this reason, delegating responsibilities is important in keeping things in order and the company busy and engaged.

Naturally, in an ensemble of people who barely know each other, insecurity, impatience, and self-centeredness are to be expected. Trust time to relieve you of such hindrances, trust actors to reveal themselves to you, and finally, trust yourself to learn by trial and error. Simon Shepherd thinks that "the relationship between the leader and the led has to be dialectical [...]. By agreeing to be observed and led, the directed allow the director to have existence. The facilitator is facilitated" (Shepherd 2012, 35). Such understanding is the basis for mutual trust. It is also valuable to know how each actor needs to be approached. Sometimes, subtle psychological manipulation will do where rigorous argumentation fails, and "one size fits all" is never a full-proof expedient. Be flexible, whether that concerns determining if it is best to have group or individual meetings after a run-through or giving more technical feedback.

Indeed, there are various tactics that directors can solicit to influence and motivate. Removing actors from a secure place by alternately complimenting and critiquing them is a strategy of maintaining focus and perspective, even if it does not always come across as a friendly act in convivial spirit. Yet, given how differently actors tend to handle instructions and criticism, conditioned by their disposition and training, you should be prepared to push a variety of buttons. You may, for instance, request physical images and coordinate improvisations for actors with a manifestly text-based approach; give initiative and elicit resourcefulness and drive from less experienced actors who wish to be told exactly what to do; or even, during select rehearsal exercises, grant protagonist's status to actors with minor parts in performance.

With all that in mind, be alert to what different people and personalities need and keep your preconceptions and common judgment errors in check. A solid training in "people management" or "amicable manipulation" can keep rehearsals efficient, appease actors' insecurities, cajole producers into higher budgets, and quietly convince collaborators that their suggestions will be adopted, when in fact everyone knows they won't. Finally, when things are tense, try to keep your cool. Many a great director has had to rely on a timely comment, a joke, or a witty icebreaker to rescue a situation that risked being marred by idleness and incompetence, malicious gossip, petty politics, or mere miscommunication. And did I mention reward? Don't forget to offer praise when someone has had a breakthrough or a moment of revelation.

Communicate Clearly	• *No matter how sophisticated the concepts you discuss, the way you communicate them must be transparent and straightforward.*
Organize	• *Set the pace of rehearsals confidently. Structure gives security.*
Lead	• *Always remember that too much containment can circumvent creativity and impulse. Too much freedom generates slackness and, eventually, apathy.*
Control, Delegate, Emancipate	• *Step back to allow for more initiative to flourish, but also remain alert to potential complications and be ready to intervene, when necessary.*
Bond, Humor and Comfort	• *Retain your sense of humor when a situation seems strained or tentative.*
Play, Challenge, Push Buttons	• *Balance between complacency and alertness. Handle tension creatively and keep performers at their toes. Force them to be more courageous. When stimulated, any artist will see challenge as an opportunity to grow.*
Show Trust	• *Have confidence in your collaborators to successfully carry out the tasks you have assigned, even if it is impossible to be entirely sure of the outcome beforehand.*

Adjust, Maneuver and Reward

- *Know that although some actors work better with reasoning and enjoy intellectual debates, others will respond to emotional triggers, encouragement and a more empathetic approach. Learn when to push, comfort, suggest or lead, when to listen, remain silent and direct by simply not directing. Once your method becomes secure, you will no longer be afraid to revise it whenever new ideas or practices come into view.*

And a final word on leadership and power. Real authority, rooted in expertise but also charisma, is the ability to persuade and influence. Contrary to authoritativeness, sometimes prompted by an unhealthy release of insecurity, it is no alibi for bullying actors and the company but a sign of respect earned gradually, grounded on an awareness of individual value. Ultimately, you practice leadership and build loyalty by communicating the force of your own commitment.

WORKBOOK 3.2

Practice I. The "Good Director" Guide

Containing fundamental directing aptitudes, the following list leads you through aspects of your method that deserve more attention.

- Create your inventory of the "ideal director's" skills and talents. Then check yourself against the different items on this list. How well do you fare?
- On what aspects of the craft do you need to work more?
- Can you spot your strengths and weaknesses?
- How can you improve? How can your group help you?

Some general areas of competence include, but are not limited to, the following:

- Making decisions fast
- Being respectful and sensitive to the needs of others
- Being organized and disciplined
- Remaining calm during mishaps

- Being reliable
- Handling conflict with dignity and cool
- Being open to ideas and willing to experiment
- Having strong interpersonal skills
- Being able to take (self) criticism
- Being resourceful and ready to make adjustments.

Practice 2. The First Rehearsal Challenge

The following checklist prepares you for the (often dreaded) first rehearsal, where people may be new to each other, the particulars of the project still unknown and the director's method of working vague to most.

Here are a few things that directors commonly do during first rehearsals:

- They introduce themselves to the company.
- They introduce the cast and the team members (producer, designers, choreographer, stage manager, dramaturg, assistant director/s).
- They describe the project, elaborating on their reasons for taking it on, and briefly presenting their basic production concept.
- They talk about their method of work (table work, sharing research, physical improvisations, etc.) and discuss the intended style of the production.
- They explain why the play is necessary at this particular moment in time and what they expect to communicate to the audience.
- They invite the set designer to talk about the idea behind the set and present a model, if it is ready.
- They initiate a first reading of the play, with everyone present in the room.
- They allow for preliminary questions regarding interpretation and point of view.
- They give actors a detailed rehearsal schedule.
- They ask the SM to circulate a contact sheet with the company members' contact details.

Of Crisis and Failing

Once directorial intentions are set within a formal frame, nothing should feel random or neglected. Directing is about taking responsibility for every single choice onstage. However, the odd chance accident should also be encouraged—theatre appears sincere and believable when pitted against the contingencies of live performance. Uncertainty and chance can apply to anything, from a severely injured knee in rehearsal to an unexpected power cut on opening night, an actor arriving late for the performance, an ill-tempered spectator who refuses to turn his or her cell phone off. Much worse, to a playwright who threatens to sue the producer and bring the show down unless a director reconsiders staging a scene in a particular way or removing an interpolated line. Where you can, use such quandaries to your advantage. Rather than ignore, accept and endorse setbacks. After all, as Lev Dodin, Artistic Director of the Saint Petersburg Maly Drama Theatre, claims,

> You have all sorts of inner doubts and you are drawing people in when you yourself do not know the road or where you will arrive. Yet, it seems that everyone must assume that you know both the road *and* the destination. If the road changes, then everyone has to see it as a discovery and not as a defeat.
>
> (Qtd in Shevtsova and Innes 2009, 61)

The Right to Fail

Failure, the (often necessary) interruption of an idea's journey to completion, is an integral stage of creativity. Most of us tend to measure leaders by their ability to overcome crisis smoothly. Naturally, some obstacles are just impossible to get past, and the earlier you accept the fact and remain in control when they break out, the better. In practical terms, you should get comfortable with failure *yourself,* to be more credible when attempting to inspire faith and tenacity in your group. Try to resolve conflict before it develops into a full-blooded fight and be quick to respond in time to prevent mishaps over the course of rehearsal or performance. The elaborate challenges of interacting with a mosaic

THOUGHT

Grappling with chaos sometimes precipitates mental clarity and a bolder perspective. Mistakes are opportunities for improvement, sheltering discoveries that can develop your ideas further.

of complex personalities, appeasing discomfort and anxiety, mitigating the pressures of technical and dress rehearsals—not to mention the terror of the opening night—require timely reflexes, admirable cool, unwavering energy and focus.

The Enemy of Literalness

THOUGHT

Always try to look at a particular scene in less predictable ways. Give yourself and your actors a chance to experiment and permission to fail. In most cases, it will pay off.

If surprise is the heart and soul of the theatre, being literal, far from referencing accuracy and authenticity, is undoubtedly one of its worst enemies. Unfortunately, even the most experienced director may surrender to the sirens of fast, opportune analogy. Because theatre operates on suggestion and leaps of imagination, although clarity is a desirable property of storytelling, literalness can make the most compelling narrative seem reductive or irrelevant.

Over-Rehearsed vs. Under-Rehearsed

THOUGHT

Carefully reconsidered challenges can bring freshness to a work that feels a little too "orderly" or stale.

As a director, you must keep an eye not just on the quality but also on the volume of rehearsing—has the production reached a point where it feels over-rehearsed? If so, you should perhaps step back and reevaluate your plan. Introduce minor changes in the blocking and give actors room to improvise generously, without, however, unsettling them to the point of confusion and invalidating their past discoveries. If on the other hand, a run-through seems under-rehearsed as a result of inadequate preparation, you need to lift up your sleeves and work with a renewed focus and greater attention to detail.

Dealing with Doubt

Sometimes, doubt sets in among company members who may feel uncomfortable with or uncertain about the way a project is shaping up. To restore trust lost along the way, you need to find ways to make things look and sound new and necessary: readdress and rethink the themes, concept, and actions of the play and refocus basic rehearsal targets.

> **THOUGHT**
>
> Directors are the actors' third eye, by-proxy spectators, who foresee what may or may not work in performance and make adjustments in rehearsal.

Facing Resistance and Lack of Motivation

There are perhaps few things more troublesome than a resistant performer or an exhausted company of actors. Resisting is another way of crying out for help, a circuitous, indirect plea for attention. There will be times, especially shortly after the first run-throughs, when the actors, tired and unmotivated, will feel stuck in one specific mode of performance. Other times, they may indulge in the immense relief that comes with having "conquered" the play, or at the very least blocked it. They will also get self-conscious and ask for constant reassurance, and their vulnerability is bound to escalate as they get closer to opening night.

> **THOUGHT**
>
> The more actors resist, the more you need to cultivate in them a sense of complicity, the understanding that they too are entitled to making choices. Break the cycle of opposition or reluctance by offering validation, where necessary.

Brace yourself against even stronger resistance and crankiness in the last phase of rehearsals, and know that, as always, this too will pass.

In Love with Ideas

Overintellectualized, "precious" concepts may have you obsess over a specific outcome in performance, which, in turn, can prevent any improvements from flowing into the work. Hanging onto an idea for too long can be an offshoot of insecurity, further aggravated by lack

> **THOUGHT**
>
> Fixed ideas and predetermined objectives will remain protected within the private sphere of your vision unless they are exposed to the critical eye of the performer and the reality of actual embodied practice.

of experience. In fact, learning from the work that develops in the company is essential. "The only thing that matters to me," says John Collins, "is the process of making discoveries in rehearsal. If that's happening, then I feel like I'm doing the right thing; if I'm learning things in rehearsal that I didn't know or maybe couldn't have known by just reading or thinking or writing" (interviewed by the author, 2016).

Self-Criticism

In times of high pressure, as is routinely the case during tech week, even the most coolheaded directors may have difficulties handling their stress. In any phase of rehearsals, managing actors' schedules, negotiating producers' demands, or facing the technicians' objections to a particular design idea, you too may lose your motivation and become dissociated from the process. Not least, because, rather than practice the art of your profession, as you no doubt wish to do, you are constrained by the logistics of production.

> **THOUGHT**
>
> In the liminal space between creativity and work exertion you may waver in your dual role of artist and facilitator, buried under a mound of exacting, dreary duties. Don't beat yourself up and brave it all out. Recognition and catharsis almost always follow a crisis, and that is not the unique prerogative of Greek tragedy!

When to Compromise

Is there a time when you should just let go and try to meet the company halfway? How long can you keep defending your choices and adamantly holding on, against general disapproval and unease? Acknowledging hard-set limitations and accepting the obvious fact that there is only this much you can push, is essential to moving on, mainly because pressure might build hard and immovable blocks, impossible to remove later on. In the long run, the main thing is to remain committed. Renew your vows to the company to eliminate accrued suspicion. This can be the first among a series of steps aimed to put the derailed production train back on track.

THOUGHT

When all else fails, when appealing to instinct and the senses won't do, you should communicate your leader status confidently, and keep the team proactive. While collaboration is a prerequisite to any success, at some point you will probably have to act as the voice of authority (Sidiropoulou 2017, 96).

WORKBOOK 3.3

Practice I. Building an Ensemble Spirit

How can you get your actors to work in harmony and operate as an ensemble? The following exercise can be an enjoyable and stimulating means of bringing the company together. Actors will need to function as directors who are nonetheless expected to collaborate with each other, argue or defend their ideas and negotiate a substantial (common) line of interpretation.

Break your actors into groups of three to five.

Present them with a situation that has strong dramatic value (a family argument, a shocking confession, a long-awaited apology, etc.), and ask them to stage it collaboratively.

Within the group, everyone should take turns analyzing their personal reading, but ultimately, the group members should all agree on one conceptual line of dramatization and of staging.

Ask each group to come up with clear choices about setting, movement, and sound, which will reflect a consistent line of interpretation.

Open up a dialogue about the challenges of working as an ensemble.

Practice 2. What Is Your Problem?

This is a technique for developing a degree of directorial self-awareness. You can better monitor your progress and handle specific flaws after you have acknowledged them in full honesty.

Whether you are an experienced professional or in the early stages of your career, there will surely be aspects of the directing art with which you feel particularly comfortable or uncomfortable. Make a checklist of those that are troublesome and be ready to address them in rehearsal. Think back to some of the major challenges you have had to face in your work, staging different plays of different styles and genres, in different theatre spaces and for different groups of audiences.

If necessary, you can set up specific targets for each rehearsal week. At the end of each week, you can review those goals and evaluate any progress made. Here are some things to watch out for:

- The overall concept—does the central metaphor you have chosen hold? Does it remain strong from scene to scene?
- Consistency in interpretation and style.
- Space—is it both aesthetic and functional? Do you make good use of it or do you sense that some dynamics remain unexplored? Does it feel too empty or too cluttered? Is there anything you can do to fix possible sightlines problems?
- Costumes—do they serve your vision of the world of the play? Do they communicate the period in which you have

chosen to work? Are they surprising and original? Do they reflect less explicit sides of the characters? Do the actors look comfortable "in their skin"?

- Visual composition in each scene—can the audience read the image you are putting across? Is it theatrically viable? Does it communicate the tensions of the scene eloquently but also coherently?
- Rhythm—does your attention as audience member lag at any point? Do you get a sense of unbearable slowness or monotone? Reversely, does it feel as though the actors rush through their words and movements? Is there anything you could do to provide more variation in the rhythm and tempo?
- Delivery of text—do we understand what the actors are saying? Are we interested to find out more about their story? Are we surprised by the manner in which specific lines are uttered? If yes, is that a problem or does it stir our attention further?

Note

1 Part of my research on the role of the director as leader led to a chapter entitled "Directing and Leadership: Endorsing the Stage to Generate Collaboration and Creativity Within Corporate Contexts," in *Playing Offstage. The Theater as a Presence or Factor in Real Life*. Ed. Homan Sidney. Lanham, MD: Lexington Books, 2017: 87–100.

WORK CITED

Baldwin, Chris. *Stage Directing. A Practical Guide*. New York: The Crowood Press, 2003.

Black, George. *Contemporary Stage Directing*. Fort Worth: Holt, Rinehart and Winston, Inc., 1991.

Chekhov, Anton. *Plays*. Trans. Elisaveta Fen. London: Penguin Books, 1959.

Cole, Susan Letzler. *Directors in Rehearsal. A Hidden World*. London and New York: Routledge, 1992.

Cook, Judith. *Directors' Theatre: Sixteen Leading Theatre Directors on the State of Theatre in Britain Today*. London: Hodder & Stoughton Ltd, 1989.

Cooper, Simon. *Brilliant Leader*. Upper Saddle River, NJ: Prentice Hall, 2008.

Genovese, Michael. "The Leadership Toolkit," in *Becoming a Better Leader*. Routledge, free eBook, 2015.

Roose-Evans, James. *Directing a Play*. New York: Theatre Arts Books, 1968.

Shepherd, Simon. *Direction*. New York: Palgrave Macmillan, 2012.

Shevtsova, Maria and Christopher Innes. *Directors/Directing: Conversations on Theatre*. Cambridge: Cambridge University Press, 2009.

Sidiropoulou, Avra "Directing and Leadership: Endorsing the Stage to Generate Collaboration and Creativity within Corporate Contexts," in *Playing Off-stage. The Theater as a Presence or Factor in Real Life*. Ed. Homan, Sidney. Lanham, MD: Lexington Books, 2017: 87–100.

Chapter 4

Director and Text(uality)

The Dramatic Text

While, traditionally, text in the theatre has been associated with the written, printable script of a playwright, usually performed in front of an audience by a company of actors, twenty-first-century-theatre textuality has been consistently expanding and deepening aside and beyond the verbal element. The notion of *text* may or may not refer to a play, a script for production, an adaptation of an existing drama, a few lines that actors have improvised in rehearsal. A playwright may or may not be there and a director can also be the writer of the script, besides functioning as the production's author. Often, an ensemble of artists will collectively devise a performance out of a theme, an idea, a picture, or some verbatim material.

In this discussion, theatre textuality is seen as an agent of performative storytelling that contains fluidity and the potential for continual re-invention. We will try to examine the role of the director in dealing both with pre-scripted plays where setting, character, and actions meet in verbal form and with theatre narratives that have been composed in diverse stage idioms. For this reason, while our emphasis will be on the director's process of understanding dramatic structure, character, and language, there is also an attempt to enter the domain of "alternative"—visual and digital dramaturgies—and consider textualities that are prominent in contemporary theatre-making, albeit not necessarily dramatic.

Reading Plays

To any director, spending time to understand how texts work is a necessary investment. To explore different interpretative possibilities you must become quite familiar with the play's givens, and in general, contribute mental and emotional capital and trust to sustain a journey that will prepare the text for its debut rendezvous with a live audience. The metaphor of a committed relationship is here cogent. Play analysis could be viewed as a series of first dates with a prospective lover, before the relationship blossoms into a condition of shared intimacy and sensitivity to each other's strengths and weaknesses, and into a mutual confirmation of interest and involvement—all of which are meant to come together in the staging phase. The two involved parties (text and director) gradually discover what it is that brings them together beyond an initial fleeting attraction and learn to adapt to meet each other's needs and preferences, often battling against moments of insecurity and doubt, stubbornness and utter incompatibility, along the way.

> Based on both logic and intuition, play analysis calls for commitment to detail and openness to free association. On that account, it is both centripetal and centrifugal—moving toward the text for clues, details, and facts, and outside of the text, for ideas that help visualize the world onstage.

Every dramatic text is in some form or another encrypted, and unlocking it is a matter of engagement and imagination. When you analyze a text, you ultimately decode its performativity, searching in the lines for those implicit elements characterized by stage potential. Understanding how a play is built and identifying its center of gravity will later on help to steer the spectator's gaze to what is essential. In fact, text analysis involves "piecing the known and unknown together into a consistent and meaningful pattern just as detectives do in crime fiction" (Thomas 2009, Xxxiii). As readers, directors are naturally privileged but also tied to strategies of unleashing connections between the abstract world of language on a page and its concrete realization onstage. Just as theatre is both a product of a literary mind and a collaboration of stage processes, theatre textuality unites the discursive and the symbolic with the material and the embodied.

Informed decisions come after a careful study of the words of the text in their autonomy but also in their interactions. As we have already suggested, for a director, being true to the text—far from prescribing adherence to some vague idea of fidelity to the playwright—is about making words resonate into a three-dimensional space, alone or in their dialogic combinations. As a director eavesdropping on situations that can happen to real people in real places, you read and interpret *texts* as opposed to the *information* that surrounds them—be it the playwright's biography or the play's historical context, production history, and critical reception—In these initial readings, you will usually keep notes of elements you find arresting in the text, with which your primary responsibility lies. Over the course of the entire production, you will no doubt return to the script again and again but also refer to other sources for your analysis.

> Studying the text is an undertaking both analytical and synthetic: you go through the information that the writer provides in the dialogue and stage directions, and then build a concept, block after block, cutting or adding lines, organizing central events, and deciding what is necessary for moving the plot onward. Along with the analysis of theme and subject, the choice of words, the way they are connected syntactically, the physical presence of the text on the page and its unique rhythmical patterns, are all clues for grasping its complexity of meanings.

In the first few days or couple of weeks of rehearsal, the company spends a period of concentrated time working on the text, what is commonly referred to as table work. Following a series of focused readings, the group will be addressing questions of subject matter, special motifs, and staging issues emanating from the text. Often, table work comes after long sessions of editing, which involve cutting lines, restructuring entire scenes, adding text or revising the phrasing and replacing words, eliminating existing characters or introducing new ones. Such changes are ordinarily made before rehearsals begin in collaboration with the dramaturg and the playwright if he or she is alive and in agreement.

> Unleashing your first, uncensored responses to the play is a crucial phase of the script analysis process. Eventually, you will make room for some distance, to evaluate the play's structural and aesthetic foundations more objectively.

Elements of Text Analysis

One of the first things to which you ought to pay attention is how defining features of specific genres are expressed in the text. For example, in dramatic works of Realism, a chain of events and reversals predictably leads up to a climactic moment in the play, soon to be followed by a "resolution." In tragedy, a powerful moment of recognition is expected to settle the anxiety that builds during the rising action of the plot and fill us with a sense of catharsis and emotional closure. In comedy, the use of timing and rhythm is paramount in delivering the textual humor. Whether you choose to emphasize, downplay, or even undermine such constitutional components, it helps to remain aware of genre-specific motifs and modes of structure.

Traditionally, plays are divided into larger or smaller units (acts and scenes, respectively), each carrying a degree of thematic autonomy. The transitions from one scene to another mark a change in plot and setting or the introduction of a new character. The principal events of each scene are structural developments that shift the story to a new direction: they advance the narrative and foster a distinct climate of feeling. One way to make sense of the play is to trace those changes one by one and decide how each scene fits into the greater storytelling arc, an integral operation of play analysis. Let us use an example from Tennessee Williams's *A Streetcar Named Desire* (1947). Williams's masterpiece tells the story of Blanche Du Bois's confrontation and ultimate defeat by the world of Stanley Kowalski, which is shockingly alien to her fragile concept of reality. In the play, each of the 11 scenes is clearly marked by an important dramatic event:

- Blanche arrives at the Elysian Fields (Scene 1)
- Blanche reveals the loss of Belle Reve (Scene 2)
- Blanche meets Stanley's friends, who are involved in a poker game (Scene 3)
- Blanche realizes Stella's changed attitude to life (Scene 4)
- Stanley confronts Blanche over her transgressive past in Laurel (Scene 5)
- A romance develops between Blanche and Mitch and she opens up about her dead husband (Scene 6)
- Stanley breaks the news about Blanche's misconduct to Stella (Scene 7)
- Blanche's birthday party turns sour, as Stanley becomes vicious (Scene 8)
- Mitch coarsely rejects Blanche, and all her expectations are broken (Scene 9)
- Stanley rapes Blanche, while Stella is at the hospital giving birth (Scene 10)
- Blanche is being led away to a psychiatric clinic, as Stanley's and Stella's life resumes its regular rhythm (Scene 11)

Play analysis usually starts with identifying the "given circumstances," which, according to Stanislavski, make up the entire situation of the play, combining the past and present-life conditions of the principal characters. To be discussed further when we examine the actor's preparation, given circumstances is basically the information that explains the characters' *milieu*, answering to a set of *wh-questions* (who, what, where, when). It can be anything from indications of geography, period, season, and time of the day to social, economic, and religious context; anything, that is, which gives the characters substance as real human beings with fully operational lives. In the example of Williams's *Streetcar*, "who" applies to the two sets of main and secondary characters: Blanche, Stanley, Stella, and Mitch as well as Eunice, Steve, Pablo, A Negro Woman, a Mexican Woman, a Nurse, a Doctor, and a Young Collector, respectively. The "what" is the dramatically salient event in each scene, as described earlier, whereas "where" concerns the location in which the plot unfolds; in this case, the Elysian Fields in New Orleans, though constant reminders of the idealized Belle Reve, and the decadent Laurel, also point to additional loci of action. Finally, the "when" of the story describes the span of time that begins with Blanche's arrival at Stella's and Stanley's household in May and ends a few months later, after the birth of their child.

Fundamental features of scene analysis include:

Analyzing theme, character, and conflict

Theme	• The governing idea of the play, *communicating a universally acknowledged condition of life or a defining attribute of human nature. A theme is suggested rather than stated explicitly and can be expressed by an abstract noun (e.g., love, justice, self-exploration, betrayal, etc.). A play can have several themes, although directors will usually commit themselves predominantly to a single one to anchor their line of interpretation (e.g.,* Oedipus Rex *is about self-knowledge,* A Streetcar Named Desire *is about the conflict between illusion and reality, and* Miss Julie *is about the battle of sexes or the conflict of social classes).*
Subject	• *The topic that the author is writing on, which answers to the question "what is this play about?" Ideally, it can be captured in one sentence (e.g.,* The Doll's House *is a play about a woman who gradually breaks free from the confines of an oppressive, matriarchal society and achieves self-knowledge).*

Message	• An overriding idea that emerges from the play, which in some way or another helps us understand it better (in Oedipus Rex such may be the notion that humans cannot escape fate).
Characterization	• The method that the playwright applies to develop character. Information in the stage directions (explicit characterization) and the dialogue (implicit characterization) directs our attention to actions, thoughts, emotions, and attitudes, which may or may not change over the course of the play. Characterization can reveal a great deal not only about basic attributes such as age, looks, profession, family ties, marital, educational and financial status, but also about an individual's ideological and philosophical outlook, aspirations, inhibitions, and so on.
Protagonist	• The person at the core of the play whose actions move the plot forward. The protagonist usually comes with a salient opponent, the antagonist, who stands as a perpetual source of resistance and conflict.
Conflict	• The tension or struggle between two (or more) opposing characters, ideas, beliefs, or ambitions (e.g., Nora's growing conflict with her social environment in A Doll's House; Willy Loman's clash with the changing society around him in Death of a Salesman). The center of gravity in all drama, it moves the plot and validates characterization. Sometimes, the central conflict is manifest in the protagonist's internal battle (e.g., Oedipus' search for truth instigates a profound inner conflict, which leads to the climax). Other times, it can be a combination of both external and internal strife.

Motivation	• What drives the characters toward a specific action.
Obstacles	• The challenges—practical (external) or psychological (internal)—that the characters face over the course of the play, which prevent them from achieving their goals. Often, an obstacle is a personality issue (e.g., Willy Loman's self-delusion and stubbornness) and the play tracks down the character's journey to overcome it.

Processing information and understanding style

Given circumstances	• The physical, temporal, social, economic, and cultural environment of the play. It is the information that makes up the entire world of the text, which the writer imparts to the reader in the stage directions and the dialogue.
Dialogue	• The conversation (verbal exchange) between the characters. It contains all the spoken text, including monologues, soliloquies, asides and choral parts, and conveys the most valid information about the story, given circumstances and relationships in the play.
Dramatic monologue	• The speech written in the first-person singular, which is delivered solely by one character of the play (usually, but not exclusively, by the protagonist or the antagonist), during which other characters can also be present onstage. It occurs in emotionally charged moments, revealing the speaker's inner thoughts, and gives necessary information about past and present events.
Imagery	• The way a writer manipulates language to create mental images and arouse sensory reactions through description.

Mood/ Atmosphere	• *The emotional temperature of the play, which generates a range of visceral responses in the reader. It is established by the juxtaposition of imagery and dialogue, attention to the details of setting and a precise description of actions.*
Tension/ Suspense	• *The escalating feelings of anxiety regarding what is going to happen next, suspense is meant to captivate the reader within an experience of continued uncertainty and apprehension about the outcome of a particular conflict.*
Emphasis	• *The point/s in the text on which the writer decides to place the weight of the storytelling.*
Contrast	• *The coexistence of conflicting angles of characterization and storytelling, which allows for diverse perspectives to emerge. Contrast makes dialogue and situation feel layered and authentic.*

Because the final purpose of analysis is synthesis, you need to look for the points where plot, structure, characterization, language, and imagery intersect, and organize any thematic and stylistic patterns that seem to affect the shape and rhythm of the play.

Elements of Dramatic Structure

In his comprehensive theory of drama, the *Poetics* (335–322 BCE), Aristotle named plot as the most important of the six elements of tragedy, over character, dialogue, idea, music, and spectacle. Plot describes the arrangement of incidents and follows a story in its sequential progress. And while story encapsulates the entire narrative arc, plot refers to the *moment-to-moment* unfolding of events. Needless to say, were we to stretch the function of plot somewhat further, we could also accommodate the characters' inner life as an important part of it; it can influence decisions that change the circumstances of the play and shift its dynamics to a different direction. At any rate, in Aristotle's theory, a strong plot must have a beginning, middle, and end, and outline a unified action with a high level of probability. The following graph illustrates a movement following the different stations of the character's journey, from an initial state of order and balance to a final resolution of the conflict or conflicts that have occurred in his or her dramatic lifespan.

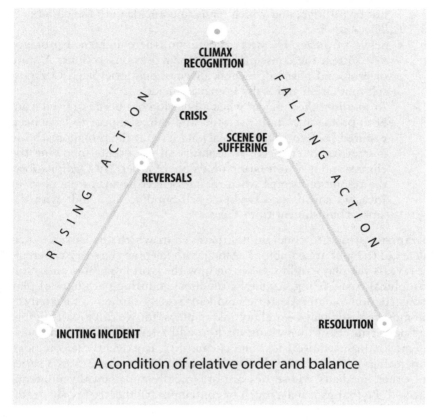

CLIMAX
RECOGNITION

CRISIS

SCENE OF
SUFFERING

REVERSALS

RISING ACTION

FALLING ACTION

INCITING INCIDENT

RESOLUTION

A condition of relative order and balance

Figure 4.1 Aristotle's Model of Plot Structure. ©Babis Melikidis

Predominant elements of Aristotle's model of structure include:

1   *A condition of relative order and balance preceding the opening of the play*
2   *Rising Action:*
    • *Inciting Incident*: an event that propels the action forward.
    • *Reversals*: a series of complications that may tip or radically influence the protagonist's course alongside an expected course of action.
    • *Crisis*: the most dramatically intense moment of the plot, when the action is approaching its resolution.
    • *Climax*: the one moment in the play where all built-up tension reaches an emotional peak.
    • *Recognition*: the knowledge accumulated throughout the rising action, which finds release in a specific moment of the play.

A state of enlightenment for the protagonist, which may or may not be positive, and which tends to coincide with the climax.

3   *Falling Action:*

- *Scene of Suffering:* after recognition, the enlightened protagonist suffers the consequences of their previous actions. A state of profound physical, mental, or emotional grief (e.g., Oedipus' self-mutilation and Willy Loman's suicide).

- *Resolution:* the moment when all tension has been removed from both protagonist and spectator, and things appear to have been restored back to a state of placidity, even if the protagonist's life is irrevocably changed. It contains all the events following the climax and is a restoration of a state of order. (In *Oedipus Rex*, the resolution begins when the messenger brings in the news of Jocasta's suicide and Oedipus' self-blinding, and ends with the latter's banishment from Thebes.)

Dramatic structure concerns the manner in which the distinct incidents of the plot are combined. Along with keeping the story coherent, it reveals the playwright's views on how the world operates on a philosophical basis. Being, arguably, the most enduring paradigm of play construction to date, Aristotle's model is widely applied to the analysis of most realistic plays—and not just to plays, for we can't really ignore its powerful effect on writing for film and television. This is no accident; Realism, whose backbone is causality, is exigently teleological, operating on the premise that each incident of the plot causes a series of other incidents whose ties are organically and logically interconnected. Be that as it may, much of contemporary theatre revisits traditional rules of structure, interrogating the validity of a sequential plot and the principles of suspense and crisis. In fact, a general problematization of linearity and causal composition has been present in theatre scholarship and practice from the mid-twentieth century onward. As British playwright David Edgar points out, play structures "fall into two categories: those using linear time and those which disrupt it" (2009, 203).

On that account, structure is "not just a convenient way of organising material, but is a conveyor of meaning" (Edgar 2009, 203). In the past, traditional lines of theory tended to reduce plays to "a series of minor crises and climaxes with intervening moments of lessened tension" (Dietrich and Duckwall 1983, 24). That perception of dramaturgy was predominant to play analysis, at least up to the middle of the twentieth century. However, the nature of crisis and climax differs significantly from one era to another. In many twenty-first-century plays, the moment of crisis is often the very space of inaction, located at the intersection of the character's assumed agency and actual impasse. As a result, conflict no longer references a spectacular clash between instantly traceable values, personalities, or desires. It can be complicated, ambiguous, and precipitous, emerging suddenly from the remotest corners of our system of beliefs. Because representational ideals in the theatre are relentlessly revised, it helps to remain sensitive to the meanings inscribed in the tissue of the play and to its building foundations. Crucial to the interpretation of any dramatic work is also the existing cultural conditions at the moment it was created.

Validated by Beckett's emblematic *Waiting for Godot* (first performed in 1953), anti-mimetic theatre, rejecting the cause-and-effect logic of Aristotelian structure, proffers randomness, accumulation, and circularity. Writing is based on suggestion and understatement rather than on denotation and clarity; also, on repetition instead of serial narrative, silence and ellipsis in place of dialogue and definitive articulation. Climaxes are often understated or even inferred, while the endings may be ambiguous and elusive. As theatre moves deeper and deeper into postdramatic expression, structure is formalized even more—it blends dialogue with epic and the narrational with the poetic. A complex, slippery, or open-ended plot development can manifest itself in a variety of dramatic models, which are sometimes hybrids—compounds of different constitutive principles—but also homocentric, having already absorbed smaller constitutional patterns. The example of *Waiting for Godot* demonstrates perfectly how structure communicates meaning: Beckett's play balances between the tragic and the comedic element, as the two roadside tramps, Vladimir and Estragon, seem forever doomed to wait for a certain "Mr. Godot," while, in the meantime, as Vladimir pronounces, "Time has stopped" (36). Beckett built his play as an exercise in perennial suffering, borrowing from French author Albert Camus's essay "The Myth of Sisyphus" (1942), which describes how, according to Greek mythology, Sisyphus, punished by the gods for tricking them, was made to roll a rock up a hill, which nevertheless always rolled back down. The play's cyclical pattern is interspersed with countless repetitions (namely, the recurrent games and the seemingly differentiated but ultimately unchanged habits of Vladimir and Estragon or the fruitless arrivals of the messenger boy). Underlining the existential futility in the heart of the play, Beckett situates the action at the antipodes of the Aristotelian dramaturgical model of "inciting incident-rising action-climax-resolution," which has served the Christian ideal of teleology. Documenting the loss of all certainties following World War II, the play emphasizes through its structure the impossibility of redemption and of closure. Time and space have been canceled. The ending is identical to the beginning:

ESTRAGON: Well, shall we go?
VLADIMIR: Yes, let's go.
  (They do not move)

(54)

VLADIMIR: Well, shall we go?
ESTRAGON: Yes, let's go.
(*They do not move*)

(93)

A refusal "to supply an ending in which all the informational discrepancies are eliminated and all the conflicts resolved"—undoubtedly a deviation from the classical norm—could, therefore, be regarded as a "the result of a changed view of what a plot should be" (Pfister 1998, 96). As a result, directors needn't base their interpretation "on a single constellation of crisis or conflict," since writing is "concerned to demonstrate a lasting condition for which a resolution or closed ending would be unthinkable" (96). Sometimes, playwrights will withhold even the most basic factual information: they will eliminate stage directions, character names and their accompanying attributes, leave location and time unspecified or refuse to formally divide the script into acts or scenes. In those instances, meaning is to be traced in this absence of connection, in the disjointed portrayal of character, the randomness of pattern, the never-ending recycling of experiences and the fragmentation of the self. Your job as director is to trace these absences intuitively and analytically, and synthesize story line, context, and character relationships, creating new associations or revealing the missing ones through the *mise-en-scène*.

Scene Breakdown: Actions, Units, Beats

Much has been made of "truthfulness" in dramatic writing, with contradictory or patronizing criticism generated from either side of the author-practitioner binary. Plays, however, don't have to present facts in a more or less "correct" manner or plausible structure. Truth, if anything, lies in the ability to stir emotion and keep alive fundamental human questions. That can be done in any form, language or structure, traditional-mainstream or unorthodox-experimental. One thing, perhaps, is universal in all good drama: there is always a degree of action and conflict, however minimal, whether pronounced verbally or hinted at in physical, visual, or digital forms.

Konstantin Stanislavski's method of script analysis, which continues to be widely applied in many phases of rehearsals, was devised to help actors build believable characters through actions and objectives. Terms such as *units* or *beats* (borrowed from Stanislavski) continue to fill some theatre artists with dread, considered obsolete in more adventurous forms of practice. Nonetheless, they are staples of actors' and directors' vocabulary, pointing to shape and dramatic focus, and leading to playable and ultimately, honest, choices in staging. We shall examine the function of Stanislavski's actions and objectives in more detail in the last chapter of the book, when we approach the subject of actor preparation. To understand the practice of play analysis a little better, we will here consider *action* from the point of view of the director's study of a scene, rather than the actor's work on developing character. Action, what characters do to achieve their objectives (what they want) in each moment of the dramatic time, encapsulates instances of recognizable human behavior, which it expresses in active (transitive) verbs.

Where should a director look for action clues? Primarily disclosed through words (in the dialogue and the stage directions), action can also be implied, hidden in suggested movement, character description, and scenographic leads. Where the action of a particular scene is not instantly visible, work with association and inference, and scrutinize every possible subtextual indicator. The same is true for objectives, the characters' needs throughout the play, which are principally manifest in their actions.

During table work, and after the themes, context and given circumstances have been determined, directors will usually break down the script into separate blocks of thematic content. Acts are the largest containers of dramatic progress, followed by scenes, which, in turn, are made up of *units*, agents of action that are separated from each other by a clear indication of change in setting, time or action. In practice, during scene analysis, you will break the larger pieces of text (scenes) into smaller divisions (units) and then divide them further into even smaller fractions of action (*beats*). Beats are in fact minuscule vehicles of meaning, clarifying each unit in detail. On the whole, scene units, like signals, mark the [actor's] channel and "keep him in the right creative line" (Stanislavski 1989, 124). Whether you are dealing with acts, scenes, units, or beats, it is advisable that you and the actors look for the motivation behind the structural divisions in the text.

In most cases, units are freestanding dramatic events whose core essence can be arrested in one single sentence (e.g., Oedipus interrogates Tiresias; Nora walks out on her past life). Being agents and containers of action, they are characterized by thematic autonomy. They also feature an organic bond with the "before" and "after" of the present moment, tracing the characters' backstory, and carrying their current energy to the future. In fact, a change in action signifies the transition from one unit to the next, and each new unit is a natural consequence of the one before it. You may find it helpful to identify units with a *subject-sentence* (a title, a catchphrase) that fitly epitomizes their principal event (e.g., Oedipus' self-mutilation; Stanley's discovery of Blanche's past; Biff's confession). Once you have pinpointed these shifts, it will be easier to grasp the theme architecture of the entire scene.

Given that the purpose of analysis is to work both in detail and with the larger shape of the scene (what Stanislavski called "through-line" of action), dividing the script into units and beats must be done with caution. Stanislavski's advice to actors (in fact, to anyone engaged in textual analysis) is telling:

> Do not break up a play more than is necessary, do not use details to guide you. Create a channel outlined by large divisions, which have been thoroughly worked out and filled down to the last detail... You ask yourself: 'What is the core of the play—the thing without which it cannot exist?' Then you go over the main points without entering into detail.
>
> (1989, 126)

A comprehensive and sensitive breakdown of the play, scene-by-scene, arbitrates its shape and rhythm, the way it moves, where it comes from and where it is going. Just as importantly, it helps you and your actors look for the character's most pressing actions and objectives, a task, which, according to Stanislavski, should be an indispensable part of rehearsals. Examining the through line of action, you invest in the characters' life.

Archetypes, Characters, Ciphers

The attempt to come up with a universal, all-inclusive definition of character is to a degree pointless since the understanding of the term inevitably follows theatre's response to representations of the human subject across time and space. Conceivably, a character is the unfolding of a person's multiple sides and contradictions in the lifespan of a text, a carrier of change across a continuum of actions. Character, as Bert O. States tells us, is so elusive because "it is at once cause and effect, both the fuel that drives the plot and a kind of exhaust or emanation given off." Characters cannot be conceived without action any more than "one can conceive of gravity without seeing objects falling through its field" (States 1985, 87). They carry their personalities, attitudes, and dispositions, but still influence the story and transform themselves and other characters by their actions. In this sense, they never exist in a vacuum but are always in some relationship with other characters, who may be present, recalled in memory or even made up. Complex characters are fluid and dynamic, impossible to pin down, carrying the ambivalence and inconsistencies of living human beings. But while they are sometimes studied as if they were real people, they can also be seen as "androids whose programming depends first upon the playwright and then upon the actor" (Thomas 2009, 168).

Sometimes, information about the characters' physical looks, their age and profession, their familial or romantic relationships, but also their particular mindset, needs and inner obstacles, is provided in the stage directions. Still, most directors know that characters are revealed primarily in the dialogue (what they say to each other, what they say about themselves, what others say about them) and in their actions (what they do). In fact, because characters are revealed in and through what they *do* (rather than what they *are*), character analysis should concentrate on actions rather than attitudes or mental and psychological attributes. In the words of David Mamet, "one can no more base a performance on an idea than one can base a love affair on an idea" and, similarly, "nothing in the world is less interesting than an actor on the stage involved in his or her own emotions" (1999, 30, 11).

Building a role is as much an understanding of character as is an exploration of one's capacities and limits as an actor. However, understanding the way a character evolves and the structural mechanisms that make progress possible—for instance, characters tend to show their true colors often during the play's most climactic scenes—is not exclusively an actor's job. It also asks of the director to imagine one character in a space with others and use point of view to foreground unexplored elements of personality as well as less obvious relationship dynamics. Which distinctive side of the character will you emphasize over others, and why? How is this focus consistent with your interpretation? In the end, how dominant is this particular character trait on the page, and would its portrayal onstage be equally commanding?

> Characters are more than the sum of their actions, personalities, and desires. They develop across a wide range of circumstances and ideally bear in them life's perturbations and inconsistencies.

In classical plays, the main characters are moral archetypes, epitomizing specific human qualities. King Oedipus is the archetype of a just ruler, Antigone is the archetype of courage and resistance, and Romeo is the archetypal lover. Surely, dramatic character becomes a lot more individualized as we move across time; nonetheless, modern characters can also achieve emblematic status, even though the heroic figures of the classical tradition are now replaced by archetypes of a different scale and nature. For example, Arthur Miller's *Death of a Salesman* (1949) depicts Willy Loman's plight as the tragedy of a layperson, of a modern-day antihero. Similarly, no matter how unique the life circumstances of Laura Wingfield in Tennessee Williams's *Glass Menagerie* (1944) are, we can still consider her condition as quintessential of social exclusion, and her, in particular, as the archetype of the outsider.

Some updated theatre history may perhaps illustrate the thrilling possibilities of character development available to directors and actors. From as early as the 1970s, characterization has taken a turn for the abstract, leading us to non-human/a-human/post-human dramaturgies, in which the materiality of the performer's body is no longer relevant. The notion of character has moved past the individual self to embrace alphabet letters, numerals, and even concepts. Already back in 1982, Beckett's television play *Nacht und Träume* (*Night and Dreams*) featured five elements (evening light, the dreamer [A], his dreamt self [B], a pair of dreamt hands, and the last seven bars of Schubert's lied) to stand in for the play's cast. In Peter Handke's *A Ride Across Lake Constance* (1971), the actual actors' names lent themselves to the characters of the play. More recently, in Oriza Hirata's *Sayonara* (2013), an android entitled Geminoid F recited poetry to a dying girl, while *I, Worker* brought together onstage two human actors and two robots. In the dramaturgy of the new millennium, a character can be a sign or a cipher suggesting presence, rather than a consummate personality of human complexity. In Simon Stephens' *Pornography* (2011), the opening stage directions state that the play "can be performed by any number of actors. It can be performed in any order" (Stephens 2009, 295). In the script of *Fewer Emergencies* (2005), Martin Crimp lists his characters as the numbers 1, 2, or 3 and describes both Time and Place as "Blank." In Sarah Kane's *Crave* (1998), the list of characters is made up of C, M, B, and A. In Enda Walsh's *Ballyturk* (2014), the characters are intriguingly announced as follows:

"Characters
1
2
3
A seven-year-old GIRL"

(Walsh 2014, 8)

Who, then, is dramatic character today? How do we map absences of the self and, more importantly, how necessary, viable, or in the end pertinent is a believable, psychologically conceived character? Is character action, situation, or pure instinct? Is character language, information, data, or a totality of fleeting impressions? Should you continue to look for or endow with human attributes nameless entities whose identifies are ever fluid?

> Whatever the genre, structure, and style, a dramatic character is a manifestation of some form or degree of cognitive movement, a person, element, or energy that undergoes change and, in the process, reveals something about the world and our position in it.

Language, Dialogue, Subtext

Reiterating the biggest cliché of all, namely, that dialogue is the heart and soul of drama, could hammer home the idea that understanding the words but also the rhythm and register of speech is fundamental to delivering a sense of credibility in performance. Dialogue, after all, is the lifeblood of drama, "the primary means by which a play implies the total makeup of its imaginative world and describes the behavior of all the characters that populate that world" (Cardullo 2015, xvi). No simple verbal interchange, it vocalizes the exchange of actions between characters who communicate different needs, one toward another. While the theatre language is both dramatic/performative (dialogue) and descriptive/diegetic (stage directions), it is in the dialogue where you should be digging for clues that can lead to more sensitive characterization and less predictable staging. Studying the amount and length of sentences and speeches for intimations about character and dramatic intensity is undoubtedly useful, but attention must also be paid to revelations that come through subtle indications in the given circumstances with regards to the characters' past, social class, educational background, habits, attitude, and dispositions.

Dialogue can deliver atmosphere and mood, affecting sensory perception through rhythm, variations in the tempo and speed of speech, repetition, pauses, or silences or an unusual application of punctuation. An emotionally loaded scene can be reflected in the way the dialogue is organized, that is, in the density or sparseness of the words and the tempo of the conversation. Fragmented speech divulges anxiety, and retrospection can be slow-moving and poetically nuanced. As a director, you need to watch for textual leads that are suggested rather than stated clearly, for thoughts that have remained incomplete, for feelings left undeclared. Indeed, as Declan Donnellan points out, "the word is only the surface of something. What's really important is what makes the word happen, which is the imagination and the belief that make the word inevitable" (qtd in Delgado and Heritage 1996, 85). Embodied dialogue operates on connotation: it marks the character's state through para-verbal communication, including gesticulation, facial expressions, intonation and pitch, and so forth.

Dramatic dialogue discloses information, exposes character, filters and focuses our attention to what is at stake, delivers theme, creates tension and mood, adds visual detail, builds patterns of imagery, and sharpens the experience of the present by revoking key moments in the past.

"Haunting" the dialogue, *subtext*, character thoughts, and motivations that never make it to the surface in verbal form, nevertheless drives the emotional energy of the moment. Subtext is that which is left unsaid but remains present as a gnawing idea behind what is voiced explicitly. To understand it, you need to look closely at the dialogue and make the necessary inferences. Harold Pinter's *The Homecoming* (1965) is a play about the struggle to dominate in a family of men (Sam, Max, Lenny, Joey, and Teddy) and the catalytic force of a woman (Ruth) who changes the power dynamics. Pinter's celebrated use of subtext is present in the following scene of Act II, where Ruth is using small talk about clothes and shoes as a flirtation tactic. Repeated pauses and ellipsis add excitement and suspense to a covert sexual game:

RUTH: I always...
      Pause
      Do you like clothes?
LENNY: Oh yes. Very fond of clothes.
      Pause
RUTH: I'm fond...
      Pause
      What do you think of my shoes?
LENNY: They're very nice.
RUTH: No, I can't get the ones I want over there.
LENNY: Can't get them over there, eh?
RUTH: No...you don't get them there.

(1965, Act II, 72)

And a note on novel forms of playwriting: for the past few decades, experimental theatre has brimmed with structures that seem to preclude any straightforward strategies of play analysis. In many instances, the orality of speech takes precedence over the craftiness of the dialogue, and characters as principal conveyors of action are reevaluated along the postmodern and the postdramatic performance paradigm.

Defying linear structure and "psychologistic" approaches to drama-turgy, twenty-first-century texts tend to be heavily de-dramatized. On occasion, traditionally conceived actants (i.e., verbal clauses) surrender to linguistic structures heavily influenced by poetry and even fiction. More and more, directors are confronted with texts that have been infused with markedly formal strategies within the play text—including musi-cal notations, excessive storytelling, heightened poeticism and melodic recurrence, neologisms, puns, songs, and gibberish, irregular grammati-cal and syntactical construction, alternating narrative angles and ample soliloquizing. Staging these texts is a stimulating challenge and one that calls for radical adjustments to traditional models of analysis.

How could a director handle, for example, the following excerpt from Caryl Churchill's *Blue Kettle* (1997), part of her dramatic diptych *Blue Heart*? In this text, language eventually disintegrates to the level of disconnected sounds to comment on the utter lack of communication among the estranged characters. Evidently, one must work on the visual element to hold the essential narrative together, but more importantly, solve the linguistic puzzle for and with the actors. If the audience is to have some grasp on the elliptical dialogue, the meaning underneath the characters' use of the replacement words "blue" and "kettle" and, to-ward the end, underneath their unintelligible guttural sounds, should be fully perceived by the actors who impersonate them:

MS. VANE: What's the kettle? Blue the kettle with her, Derek?
DEREK: She gets like this, I'm kettle, she gets confused.
ENID: I can't let you believe it, he does this, he goes round kettle women and he blue it's him, he does that.
DEREK: She might be a little jealous because ever since I found you I've blue a blue preoccupied and –

(Churchill 2008, 118)

And, later, as the play reaches its finale:

MRS PLANT: T t have a mother?
DEREK: K.
MRS PLANT: B happened b k?
DEREK: Tle died ket I ket a child.
MRS PLANT: Bl bl ket b b b excuse?
DEREK: Ket b like. Or not.

(127)

In this case, scene analysis is less about determining subtext and more the decoding of a baffling language game. Having solved the riddle, you can then guide actors and spectators through the adventure of the play.

WORKBOOK 4.1

Practice 1. Analyzing Plays

The following exercises apply basic strategies of play analysis on different texts.

Activity 1. Applying a Model of Play Analysis

In your play of choice, apply the model of play analysis we have discussed, identifying theme, subject, message, and conflict. The following is an example from Chekhov's Uncle Vanya.

Theme	• *Fatalism, missed opportunities, unfulfilled dreams, dismay, and futility.*
Subject	• *Uncle Vanya is a play that portrays the existential distress of a group of well-to-do people in a countryside estate of nineteenth-century Russia, each of whom experiences a different kind of disillusionment.*
Message	• *A possible message of the play might be that people need to become bolder and take more risks, to avoid being haunted by suppressed desires and missed opportunities.*
Given Circumstances	• *The action takes place in the Russian countryside at the end of the nineteenth century. Chekhov's provincial middle-class characters are trapped by their inaction. There is an undercurrent of social upheaval, soon to instigate the October Revolution of 1917.*
Characterization	• *Unable to react against the social conventions of their time, the play's protagonists (Uncle Vanya, Sonya, Yelena, and Astrov) remain imprisoned in the daily grind and their profound boredom.*
Protagonist	• *Depending on your point of view, any one of Vanya, Sonya, Yelena, or Astrov could be the protagonist of the play. However, Vanya remains the principal thematic pivot and duly lends his name to the title.*

Atmosphere and Mood	• At times somber and wistful. Autumn in the countryside. A sense of decay. Provincial life, habit, and repetition. A mood of despondency and suffocation.
Conflict	• There are multiple conflicts: the individual vs. the self and personal ambitions (Vanya, Sonya), the individual vs. the environment (Astrov, Serebryakov), and the conflict between individuals (Vanya vs. Serebryakov; Vanya vs. Maria Vasilievna).
Objectives and Obstacles	• The characters' lives vanish among unfulfilled dreams. The social reality around them changes, while they remain deadlocked in their own little world, terrified of the changes they are also craving.
Dramatic Tension-Suspense	• There is no real suspense in the play and the tensions are mostly internal. Similarly, there is no conspicuous dramatic climax. The characters seem to wait for some vague event that will give meaning to their lives, but which is, nevertheless, not happening.
Dialogue	• The dialogue is intensely psychological. It contains extensive monologic parts that reveal each character's conflicts and that seem to provide release of pent-up distress.
Imagery	• The play matches our conception of dull provincial routine. Most images concern the interior of the family estate, gloomy and claustrophobic. One senses a heavy winter approaching, and there are also references to storms. However, there seems to be an opening into the great outdoors as well, which is visible in Astrov's descriptions of the Russian forests. The allegorical quality of the woodland is marked by nostalgia for a past during which people were in closer contact with their natural environment.

Contrast

- *The play is characterized by a series of antitheses: between expectation and reality, the hope for a fulfilling life and its cancelation. This contrast is present in the dialogue and monologues, adding to the all-embracing desolate mood.*

Activity 2. Working with Genre

In Tennessee Williams's *A Streetcar Named Desire* examine the genre of Poetic Realism and identify the structural and aesthetic motifs that characterize vital moments in the text.

- How is Poetic Realism manifest in the structure of the play?
- How is Poetic Realism revealed in language and characterization?
- How does Poetic Realism feature in the play's stage directions?
- What is uniquely poetic in this play regarding atmosphere?
- How does the presence of musical cues accentuate the poetic element?

Activity 3. Understanding Conflict

In August Strindberg's *Miss Julie* (1888):

- Decide on the main conflict that runs through the entire play.
- Specifically, identify the principal conflict for both *Miss Julie* and her valet Jean. To what extent is the nature of the characters' conflict external or internal? Practical or emotional? What elements will you take into account in your attempt to define it?
- If Julie is the protagonist, who is her antagonist and why? If the (obvious) answer were her valet, Jean, would it be worth expanding the conflict territory to her immediate surroundings (the Count, the villagers, household servants, etc.) or even to something less concrete, as is her family upbringing?

Practice 2. Clarifying Dramatic Structure

To understand the mechanisms by which dramatic structure unlocks theme and character, try to examine how playwrights from different periods and genres organize their plot to unravel action credibly and dynamically, while also making a personal statement about the protagonist's position. The following example is from Sophocles' tragedy Oedipus Rex *(430 BC), generally acknowledged to the prototype of Aristotelian plot structure.*

King Oedipus searches for the murderer of King Laius, to rescue the city of Thebes from its curse. As the events of the story unfold, Oedipus investigates the City's and his own family's past, gradually having to confront the horrible truth that causes the climax of the play: that the murderer of Laius and, therefore the curse of Thebes, is none other but himself.

Activity I. Aristotle's Ideal Plot

Establish the main elements of structure in the play, considering the following:

- What is the function of the expository scene, when the Chorus of the Elders approaches Oedipus for help?
- What is the inciting incident and how does it set the rising action going?
- Which specific items of information (reversals) complicate the plot?
- What mechanisms does Sophocles use to build up suspense and lead us to the climax?
- When exactly does the audience experience the highest moment of crisis and when does the climax of the play occur? How does the reader/spectator experience the emotions of pity and fear?
- Does the scene of suffering that follows the climax do justice to Oedipus' status of a tragic hero?

Activity 2. Dramatic Climax

Focus on Scene 10 (known as the "rape scene") of Williams's *A Streetcar Named Desire*, tracing, moment-to-moment, the acceleration of dramatic tension that leads up to Stanley's assault on Blanche. In exploring the steps that have led to the climax, you may need to work your way backward to the beginning of the scene.

- Can you recognize the climax of the scene?
- What are the separate units and beats leading up to the climax?
- How do the characters' actions influence the climax?
- How is suspense built? What means—dialogue clues, imagery, mood, rhythm, etc.—does Williams employ to bring about the climax?
- What happens to the characters in the particular moment of the scene's climax? Does the event of the climax affect their behavior in the following and final scene of the play?

Activity 3. Subverting Aristotle: The Modern Cyclical Structure

Apply the elements of scene analysis we have discussed on Beckett's *Waiting for Godot*. In this emblematic tragicomedy, Vladimir and Estragon make a promised—and as it appears, a never-to-be—visit by a so-called Mr. Godot the focus of their life and a predominant mechanism for survival in a hostile universe. Think about the significance of structure in the context of Existentialist philosophy, which gives the play its thematic pivot. Be sure to consider the exceptional similarity of structure in the two acts of the play.

- How does the play's structure reflect Beckett's nihilistic outlook?
- What does the mirroring of the two acts signify?
- How can you use the pseudo-linear frame (the expectation of Godot's arrival, the arrival of Pozzo and Lucky and the Messenger boy) to make an even stronger point about the play's lack of *telos* (in the sense of ending, but also, of purpose)?
- Can you further support the play's cyclical and open-ended dramaturgy with aspects of staging (handling of set and lighting, actors' movement, rhythm, etc.)?

Activity 4. Beckett vs. Aristotle

Compare and contrast *Oedipus Rex* and *Waiting for Godot* from the point of view of plot structure. Try to address as many of the elements in the structure chart as possible.

- Do you see any broader patterns emerging from the parallel analysis of the plays? Is there a climax as such in *Waiting for Godot*? Any sense of enlightenment (recognition) for Vladimir and Estragon? Could it be said that Beckett's text plays havoc with Sophocles' ideal plot structure—as praised by Aristotle?
- Consider how and why the fundamentals of traditional plot structure, such as rising action, complications, and reversals, climax, recognition, scene of suffering, and falling action, whose presence is paramount in *Oedipus Rex*, are in *Waiting for Godot* altogether undermined.

Practice 3. Given Circumstances

The following exercises address the significance of stage directions. They encourage you to work analytically and consider all the clues that the playwright has provided in the opening lines, which introduce the dialogue parts. They also urge you to think about how you will be using this information in performance.

Activity 1: Reading Stage Directions

In Arthur Miller's *Death of a Salesman,* concentrate on the opening stage directions of each scene. Think about how they

- Define the historical, social, and economic context in which the play is set.
- Define place (country, city, and neighborhood).
- Establish time (past and present) and communicate crucial moments of the characters' past.
- Contribute to the emotional environment of the play, as experienced by each character.
- Reveal mood, as it changes from scene to scene.

Activity 2. *Visualizing Stage Directions*

Reread the stage directions of Act I in *Death of a Salesman*, which describe Willy Loman's house and the general historical and social setting of the play, but also familiarize us with Willy's personality and his relationship with his wife, Linda. After mentally picturing Willy's presence in that specific environment, pay attention to the following:

- Do the stage directions indicate any movement?
- How do the stage directions enter the realm of characterization?
- Which stage directions will you keep and why? How do they clarify or add to your vision about the play?
- Which stage directions will you discard, if any? Justify your reasons for leaving them out.
- Which stage directions would you like to reorder or perhaps "tweak," and why?

Practice 4. Background Story

This writing exercise and the physical improvisation that goes with it offers a simple way to look for any missing links in the history of the play. It is also an opportunity for envisaging a kind of closure where you feel it is lacking, and putting an interpretive finish to the story. This kind of activity would be an interesting challenge for more experimental plays, as well.

Think of a play that provides little expository information on the characters' past or one whose ending is inconclusive. Write in your version of the "before" and "after" scenes, after you have had your actors physically improvise them.

Practice 5. Language and Rhythm

The purpose of the following activity is to make you think more about the acoustic atmosphere you are after and experiment with different rhythms, speed, and expressiveness of speech to produce surprising delivery and heighten emotional impact.

Choose a piece of dialogue from your play of choice. Decide on the prevailing mood that emanates from the specific style in which it is written (*diction*). What does each character's choice of words reveal about them?

Rewrite the dialogue, using different words and different line structures and rhythm. If you are fluent in another language, translate the excerpt and have a native speaker (preferably an actor) read it out loud.

Do you notice any changes in the rhythm?

Compare how the same scene sounds in different languages: is the sensory impact similar? How does the emotional energy of the scene change?

Practice 6. Title and Theme

Although simple, this activity can produce alternative readings and resolve point of view tersely and speedily (see also "Titling" Workbook 2.3 in Chapter 2).

Consider the title provided by the playwright in your play of choice.

Think of how it serves the play and whether it directs the audience's focus to what you consider to be its central theme.

Having settled on your narrative angle, decide if you would like to keep the title or change it.

Give a list of alternative titles that would better suit your line of interpretation.

Practice 7. Scene Breakdown

Following are two exercises in scene analysis, applied on Ibsen's A Doll's House. *They are staples of table work and can be used in any play.*

Activity 1. Determining Actions and Objectives

In Ibsen's *A Doll's House* (1879), concentrate on Act III, and, specifically, on the play's final scene, from the moment Nora's husband Torvald tries to convince her that everything is now re-solved, and burning Krogstad's contract, all through to the play's dramatic ending. Having gained an epiphany about her hollow marriage, Nora announces to Torvald her decision to leave him and her family behind to start a new life as an emancipated, inde-pendent woman. This happens after she sees Torvald's true colors and witnessing his selfish reactions to Krogstad's letters.

- Break down the scene into units and further into beats, justifying your choices. Then, decide the objectives and actions of each character in each unit of the scene and give these units titles.

There are approximately seven units in the final scene of the play, each tracing a different phase in the interaction between Nora and Torvald: (1) Torvald's changed—elated—attitude toward Nora and the burning of Krogstad's bond; (2) Torvald's "forgiving Nora" for her careless behavior; (3) Nora's changing out of her fancy-dress costume, while Torvald continues to treat her condescendingly; (4) Nora's speech about her newly gained self-awareness and her an-nouncement about starting a new life; (5) Torvald's dismay and sus-tained arguments, meant to dissuade her from leaving; (6) Nora's final tirade, upon which she leaves the house; and (7) Torvald's being left behind, hearing the door slam shut.

The characters' unit objectives flesh out their directly clashing scene objectives, which are the following:

- Torvald wants to restore the order back to his household.
- Nora wants to leave her past behind and start a new life as an independent woman.

Activity 2. Transitions and Shifts

Still working on *A Doll's House*, have your actors examine the quality of transitions between the play's three acts and the different scenes of each act.

What has changed from one act/scene to the next, besides the obvious passage of time, the different physical setting and the introduction of other characters?

Is there any inner movement, even if slight, which marks those shifts?

How does the protagonist, Nora, develop from scene to scene?

How fast or slow has the plot advanced? What is the rhythm and pacing of the change?

How inevitable does the ending appear? Has Ibsen prepared us adequately for the final *coup de théâtre*?

Practice 8. Who Is the Character in the Play?

The following two exercises address directorial attitudes to character, conceived either traditionally (Activity 1) or unconventionally (Activity 2).

Activity I. Staging Character

In *Oedipus Rex,* consider how the title character's monumental self-realization will affect your overall staging.

- Are there any aspects of the character that could be further emphasized by delivery, movement, or design?
- How will Oedipus' epiphany, his exemplary movement from ignorance to knowledge, be mirrored in his physical position onstage?
- How will you settle his posture and his costume? Will you give the actor a specific gesture following the recognition scene? An added moment of music or silence?

Activity 2. Unexpected Characters

In Beckett's minimalist text *Breath* (1969), the stage elements of lighting and sound assume character properties.

- Who are your protagonists and antagonists? Is there a conflict between them?
- What would your "characters" say if they could speak? Give each of them a suitable line.
- Could a potential staging of this playlet evolve beyond a whimsical exercise in coordinating image and sound?

Practice 9. Dialogue and Subtext

The following exercises deal with special issues in dialogue and subtext.

Activity 1. Dialogue as Engine

In your play of choice, discuss the most significant moments in the dialogue, which support the main dramatic event.

- How does language reveal character and situation?
- Are there any specific lines that seem to motivate the character?
- How is the language used to create moments of tension or release?
- How is the language used to express conflict and to contrast one character with another?
- What linguistic and paraverbal means does the playwright employ to communicate the different characters' personalities, class, education, level of comfort and emotional state?

Activity 2. Dialogue and Character

In Williams's *A Streetcar Named Desire*, pay attention to the dialogic exchanges between Blanche and Stanley across the different scenes of the play. Discuss how language generates imagery, style, rhythm, and characterization. Note how differently Williams depicts Blanche and Stanley linguistically to comment on their very distinct cultural and educational backgrounds. How will you, as a director, use, eliminate or accentuate the contrast between the two characters? Will you be applying different accents (Southern or Polish)?

Activity 3. Working with Elliptical Texts

Guide your actors through the linguistic abstraction and elliptical style of Caryl Churchill's *Blue Kettle*, and invite them to solve its semantic riddle together. As an exercise, dedicate a part of the rehearsal to going over the final scene of the play. Ask the actors to improvise the ending, filling out the missing text in any way they see fit. Then have them work out the exact words behind each of the fragments. Once they are confident they know what each broken up line, word or letter stands for, they should be able to communicate the story accurately, using rhythm, emotional cadence, movement, and gesture.

Activity 4. Reading between the Lines

Harold Pinter's memory play *Old Times* (1971) tells the story of an enigmatic love triangle between two women (Kate and Anna) and one man (Deeley), blurring the borders between reality and fantasy. Concentrate on Act II, examining the playwright's ability to imbue language with complex psychological content. Reflect on the forceful manipulation of silences and on whatever remains unsaid in the dialogue.

- Find out what is not verbally happening but is still very much present in the general mood of the scenes. Is there any missing information? What facts can we deduce from the dialogue? What is the dramaturgical function of those relationship dynamics that are never made explicit but still influence the development of the plot?

- How does subtext operate? What kind of an atmosphere does it evoke? Does it fill in for obscure moments in the story? In what way does it reflect the inner action? How is character revealed in those moments when nothing is said?

A Word on Alternative Dramaturgies

[Dramaturgy is] the process by which a playwright presents a series of acts, inner actions, revelations, changes in attitude and thought processes so as to create climaxes and reliefs.

(Cohen and Harrop 1974, 32)

Dramaturgy involves everything, is to be found in everything and is hard to pin down. It is only possible to think of dramaturgy in terms of spoken theatre, or is there a dramaturgy for movement, sound, light, and so on, as well? Is dramaturgy the thing that connects all the various elements of the play? Or is it, rather, the constant dialogue between people who are working on a play together? Or is it about the soul, the internal structure, of a production? Or does dramaturgy determine the way space and time are handled in a performance, and so the context and the audience, too? We can probably answer all these questions with "Yes, but..."

(Kerkhoven 1994, 8–10)

After an examination of the fundamentals of play analysis, we can briefly revisit, as so many other artists and scholars have done, the ever-controversial matter of what constitutes *text* in the theatre. Perhaps one of the most used, overused, and even abused terms in the realm of theory and practice, text continues to precipitate an avalanche of issues central to theatre-making and the ethics of directing and spectatorship. Because of theatre's polyphonic nature, interpretation is always dual, integral to both text and performance. In other words, being the combination of linguistic and nonverbal components that build up to a coherent narrative line, textuality is not limited to the dramatic script but extends to several other dramaturgies (physical, digital, visual, and other). Increasingly, in the twenty-first century, the democratization of meaning has established a non-hegemonic understanding of the audience's authoring involvement in the scripting of the performance, to which directors, playwrights, and actors are all entitled.

As an operation of creating texts, dramaturgy transcends the verbal script *per se*. Being a process, it is fluid and dynamic, subject and vulnerable to the intrusion of the authentic experience, the establishment of different normativities, emergent, updated or enriched artistic and critical practices. In this sense, it is always in motion, always performative, never static.

Today, spectators are more accustomed to alternative, "porous" dramaturgies, art forms that are uncomfortable, discontinuous, destabilizing, frenetic, allowing for new information, theories, and discoveries in science and technology to enter the domain of dramaticity. While traditional notions of authorship are still being scrutinized, unconventional performance environments framed by the proliferation of intermedial forms, intercultural theatre-making and a variety of human and non-human (im)materialities have advanced the disinterment of the dramatic text within the performance. Concerning narrative structure, hierarchies of causality and stability are dismantled, ushering in a sense of open-endedness, disconnection, and fluidity. This also marks a shift in the engagement and evaluation of theatrical texts, which requires a more involved function of the audience. All in all, full-proof narrative structures are jettisoned in favor of interdisciplinary discourses and practices. These "new" dramaturgies—categorically hyphenized or conflated—often operate as a bridge that connects writing with the *mise-en-scène*.

In this diverse continuum of practices, theatre artists are forced to position themselves critically and imaginatively. Instead of reductive dichotomies and collisions prohibitive to a meaningful intercourse between tradition and innovation, directors are now aiming for encounters and interactions, a kind of "conciliatory" theatre-making mode that Peter Boenisch calls "relational dramaturgy" (in Trencsenyi and Cochrane 2014, 227). And just as playwrights must now redefine their role and creative contribution to theatre-making, directors also entertain a variety of interpreting possibilities.

Although directors are mediators, who animate the playwright's interpretation of the world, they are also expected to be adventurous. They rely less and less on pre-scripted texts to generate their own devised narratives, in which, distinctions among the verbal/dramatic element, movement, imagery, and technology, are obliterated. Further empowered by the digital manipulation of sound, video, and mobile phone technology and the omnipotence of social media communities, new textualities—simultaneously dramatic and performative—are authored by ensembles and directors whose synthetic practices are momentous contributions to twenty-first-century theatre's multidisciplinarity.

Visual Text or Directextuality

The arrangement of images onstage is a different narrative that works autonomously and *not* alongside the dialogue. To set the record straight, visual dramaturgy does not rule out verbal expression. Operating as a "fusion of form and content in an embodied, if fleeting world" (McBurney quoted in Mitter and Shevtsova 2005, 250), it privileges the impressionistic and creates lasting visceral associations. Often, the story unfolds as a storyboard developed onstage. Images carry in them high interpretative significance, and by reordering or juxtaposing them in different compositions, you can produce structures of storytelling that are often just as, if not more, eloquent than words. A flair for visual imagery is at the very least a mark of a good director.

A resonant image is, however, more than a "pictorial representation or *coup de théâtre*" (Williams in Mitter and Shevtsova 2005, 250), and distancing visual techniques create emotionally fraught moments, particularly when dialogue, action, and context appear to stand in opposition to each other. Framing, the manipulation of visual configurations and elements of staging, becomes a rudiment of dramatic composition. In the same vein, a painterly perspective, 3D spatiality, and an emphasis on pictorial composition cultivate visual environments that abandon conventional storytelling devices for an invocation of atmosphere and mood. These environments naturally posit perceptual challenges on the audience, ordinarily schooled to process performance in more conformist terms. There will be more to say about how visual efficacy is achieved in the following chapter, which analyzes the director's work on set, costume and lighting design.

Visual dramaturgy is a practice that transcends the inspired selection of aesthetically pleasing moments onstage. Striking composition notwithstanding, the imagistic layering of the *mise-en-scène* can create astonishing connections between text and subtext and shed more light on characterization and story.

Visionary conceptualists, in the likes of Wilson, Mnouchkine, Suzuki, Castellucci, McBurney, Bogart, Ostermeier, Lepage, Mitchell, and van Hove, to name but a few, are renowned for their ability to create visual performances of eloquence and intense, visceral energy. Together with an increasing number of younger and much promising artists, they stretch boundaries and definitions further and further. Compiling a list of such iconoclasts here would be utopic; detailed references to notably imagistic practitioners would divert attention from our main point of focus, which is to encourage experimentation with the rich and ever-transformative nature of dramaturgy—both as text and as text-making operation. That being said, given the evolution of the concept and practice of dramaturgies that are both shaped by and are shaping performance, we could argue that theatre textuality might conceivably be served better by a new terminology in which the word "drama" is no longer present. In fact, we may need a different vocabulary altogether, a word or phrase to describe a sensory stage pushed beyond its limits: an *écriture corporelle* (Mallarmé 1970, 304), and a kind of *poetry in space*, to draw on Artaud's view of the ideal *mise-en-scène*, a *directurgy* or *directextuality*.

How does analysis change when the verbal text takes second stage? What exactly is being analyzed? When all is said and done, we should revise the examination of contemporary dramaturgy not in terms of traditional analysis but as an application of composition and synthesis. Or, perhaps, acknowledge that analysis and synthesis can periodically coincide.

Digital

How is then dramaturgy—an operation of theatre that describes both narrative composition and structure—changed in a world ruled by technology? How is technology adding to the ever-growing number of the so-called "new/alternative dramaturgies" to which we have already referred? Is intermediality a more enriched form of textuality, a substitute for language-based communication? How complex is the coexistence onstage of the live and the mediated and what is the director's position as a mediating agency—pun intended—between the drama of words and that of digits?

The transformed notions of theatre textuality have contributed to a radical shift in the understanding of theatre practice as strikingly interdisciplinary, in constant dialogue with the social and cultural realities of its times. Twenty-first-century theatre, located at the intersection of drama with production and information technologies, has ushered in new, hyphenated performative practices and forms of spectatorship.

For many auteurs, the media aesthetic largely informs the nature of storytelling. Van Hove, McBurney, Mitchell, Ostermeier, and Lepage, for example, are keen advocates of the use of technology in performance. Intermedial influences are even more pervasive in theatre companies such as the Wooster Group, Blast Theory, The Builders Association, Gob Squad, Big Art Group, Rimini Protokoll, and Invisible Flock, among others, who use video and film to experiment with the boundaries of the live and the digital component. These companies employ interactive art forms that combine performance with digital broadcasting, telepresence, online video streaming, video games, and smartphone applications.

While the understanding of *mediaturgy*[1] is too broad to settle in a brief section of this discussion on director and text, a reference to a few instances of digital textuality might be worth bringing in, if only to demonstrate the capacious scope of the directing art. To use some examples: in SUPER VISION (2005–2006), New York-based performance and media company The Builders Association examines how technology and, more specifically, 3D digital media, intersects with the visual arts and architecture. This work bridges the human and the digital element, interweaving three stories that focus on the precarious nature of human identity on "the edge of the datasphere." The presence of technology onstage is a powerful statement about the blurring of boundaries—especially of those between our known physical reality with cyberspace. This statement is brought to the fore in a series of video chats, most notably in those of Jen, a United States resident, who tries to archive digitally her grandmother's life in Shri Lanka. According to the company, SUPER VISION "explores the changing nature of our relationship to living in a post-private society, where personal electronic information is constantly collected and distributed" (http://www.thebuilders association.org/prod_supervision_info.html). Similarly wishing to engage a "diverse public through diverse means," British company Blast Theory has systematically produced art that brings live audiences into a condition of technology. As early as 2001, in the production *Can You See Me Now*, online players compete against members of the company on the streets. Tracked by satellites, Blast Theory's runners appear online next to a player on a map of the city. On the streets, handheld computers showing the positions of online players guide the runners in tracking this player down (info in http://www.blasttheory.co.uk/projects/can-you-see-me-now/). Along similar lines, British-German group Gob Squad combines audience interaction with real-time editing, operating mostly in urban spaces and art galleries (info in http://www.gobsquad.com/about-us), while New York City-based Big Art Group investigates revised modes of communication in an environment of video cameras, algorithms, social media sites, and data collection. In their celebrated *SOS* (2008), "a multi-camera and multi-screen forest of technology located within a landscape of refuse give the audience a corrupted panoptic view of colliding narratives."

Unlike traditional theatrical performance, Big Art Group's wide-ranging mediated performances reposition viewers as active editors, challenging audience members to problem-solve complex issues of sexuality, race, narrative, and truth as a theatrical mirror to the process of navigation through contemporary society (info in http://bigartgroup.com/).

What shall we call the director of these new dramaturgies? Could *theatre composer* be more suitable for our purposes or would the term *auteur* (to borrow from French film criticism) or, simply, *creator* (to remember Artaud) capture the director's revised as well as enhanced role? Whether or not their title changes, a major challenge for contemporary directors becomes how to accommodate new skills and sensibilities to respond to the speed of technology and the omnipresence of science in our daily lives.

WORKBOOK 4.2

Practice I. Technology as Character

The following exercise invites different staging possibilities instigated by the use of technology.

Stage the Willy-Howard scene from Miller's *Death of a Salesman*. Willy visits Howard's office to convince him to transfer him back to New York. While Willy is pleading, Howard shows off his new recorder to him.

- Have the performer impersonating Willy carry the drama of the scene onstage with no words.
- Remove the character of Howard and use a technological device (e.g., a radio, a mobile phone, or a video screen) to act as the voice of Willy's opponent.

Rewriting and Adapting

An adapter has to be 100 per cent faithful not to the letter of the original but to the impulse that motors the whole thing forward... adaptation is like using a foreign plug. You have to find the adaptor which will let the electricity of now flow.

(Icke in Clapp 2015)

An increasing number of directors have turned to adaptation and re-writing of existing dramatic material (for the most part, classical plays) as a way to render alive popular narratives. For some, adaptations serve the educational function of making old texts familiar to new audiences, bringing the former as close as possible to the present. For many, the practice of adaptation, which has in fact been in operation since antiquity, when the three Greek tragic poets started to recycle old myths, seems to legitimize directorial choices that would remain mostly unacceptable in mainstream theatre. The startling stories of Antigone and Oedipus, the communal plight of the Trojan women, the archetypically human or social conditions that permeate the tragedies of *Macbeth* or *King Lear* have been revised and reshaped for the stage in different ways across time and cultural contexts. Describing his process of adapting classical texts for the stage, John Collins argues that what you start with is just looking for a theatre to emerge. In the end, "when you do that in an honest way and if you don't have an agenda of destroying the original text but don't have an agenda of revering it either, it will survive" (2016).

How can classical plays be staged to feel *contemporary* as opposed to *ephemeral*?

Should directors care about the audience's expectations when it comes to adaptation?

What kind of material lends itself more smoothly to a new reading of an old text?

Are some plays better suited for certain geographical communities and different societal conditions?

Daring directors ultimately create intelligent adaptations, without necessarily rewriting the entire text but often reframing setting, period, language, movement, and action in a new light, to attune the classic to the rhythms of today. In reality, as an adaptor, you ultimately propose new artistic and affective criteria. The frontiers of interpretation are virtually limitless, eclipsing the imagined conditions of an era that may seem of little relevance or interest to your audience.

In point of fact, you can't help but consider the community of spectators your adaptation addresses. Often, the audience is bound to be at home with the original literary piece and, on occasion, with some of its previous inter- or intra-medial/temporal transcriptions. At the same time, interpretations that appear trivial or blasphemous to one audience may be appropriate to another, reflecting, as they do, some of its unique cultural conditions. Discussing the viability of adaptations using an analogy from the theory of evolution, adaptation theorist Linda

Hutcheon argues that "stories do get retold in different ways in new material and cultural environments." Like genes, "they adapt to those new environments by virtue of mutation—in their 'offspring' or their adaptations. And the fittest do more than survive; they flourish" (2006, 32). Such optimism feels warranted and seems to suggest that you can trust your instinct to tell the same known stories or stage the same popular plays in ways that may at first strike an odd chord. In the end, these approaches can prove surprisingly felicitous. Establishing your barometer of pertinence and developing mechanisms for measuring the level of appositeness of the original material to situations and attitudes familiar and meaningful today can be a useful way of approaching the practice of adaptation.

Fundamental principles and rules of adaptation include:

- Defining the updated context of the play.
- Removing or restructuring existing scenes or interpolating new ones.
- Eliminating existing characters or adding new ones.
- Adding *found* text, verbatim material, songs, and so forth.
- Examining archaic or period conventions (e.g., the function of the Chorus and the use of masks) and deciding on the production style.
- Choosing the right metaphor that makes sense in the context of the play and the production. Checking how flexible it is to support your performance.
- Establishing an energetic connection between the original text and its adaptation in terms of plot, physical setting, and characters.
- Dealing with language particularities, commissioning new translations and making adjustments to achieve a sense of contemporary, natural speech.

There are several issues that continue to problematize the slippery boundaries between staging, interpreting or rewriting, and establishing artistic agency as well as ownership of the text. Even as the debate on adaptation and the ethics of directing continues to hold firm, more and more directors today seem ready to restore a long-misplaced responsibility: that toward the text rather than the person who produced it.

WORKBOOK 4.3

Practice 1. Updating

Updating a classical play's historical context and geographical setting is one of the most popular mechanisms for bringing the work to the present.

Activity 1. Recontextualizing Plays

Consider carefully and then try to stage the principal dramatic event of Euripides's play *Trojan Women* (415 BCE) from the point of view of the contemporary refugee crisis.

- If you wished to make direct references to the present, where would you relocate the action? Who would be your characters?
- Rewrite Hecuba's lamentation, by taking into account the calamitous war in Syria and the growing asylum-seeking populations. How does the language change to accommodate current-day perspectives?
- How can you involve a twenty-first-century audience in the plight of the Trojan women, as described by Euripides?

Activity 2. Reworking/Adapting

Look for ways to build a new choral song based on the presence of the Chorus in Aeschylus' *Suppliant Women* (463 BCE) or Euripides' *Trojan Women* or *Hecuba* (424 BCE).

- Place the song in a scene taken from your adaptation of the play. Your reading should try to illuminate the experience of dislocation/migration/being in transit in the twenty-first century.
- You may then assign lines or excerpts of text to different people and build a choral rhythm.
- You may also try to involve your audience actively, giving them lines to speak, a specific placement in space, or a particular gesture that communicates a special role in the situation you've built.

Activity 3. Revitalizing Archaic Conventions

In *Oedipus Rex* examine the presence of the Chorus of the Elderly and study their function as representatives of the public voice.

Imagine relocating the play to the present time. What elements of the Chorus would you keep in a revisionist production? How would you update the Chorus to make it more relevant to our time?

Practice 2. Involving the Audience

This exercise explores the themes of civic consciousness and participatory democracy, which are seminal to the trilogy of Aeschylus' Oresteia (458 BC), and calibrates the role of the spectator as an involved citizen both in the ancient times and today. Further to bringing the whole group together, as its members become both performers and spectators for each other, it suggests different ways in which audience perspectives can be employed to highlight the predominant theme of the text.

Divide the actors into groups of four or five. Hand out copies of the trial scene in *Oresteia*'s *Eumenides* (fourth episode), which is set at the High Court of Athens. Depending on the size of the class, there should be a maximum of four groups, to allow for an adequate feedback session at the end of the exercise.

For better use of time, a short (approximately 1') excerpt of the scene would be the ideal material for this performance exercise. Concentrate on the dynamic interrogation between the Chorus of Furies and Orestes, up until the moment when Apollo addresses the Court. Each group should work independently before presenting three different versions of the excerpt, engaging the audience alternately in the following functions: (a) as the Athenian jurors who will decide on Orestes' fate, (b) as the Furies who persecute Orestes, and (c) as a twenty-first-century audience of Press critics reviewing the production. Each group member is to perform one of the main characters (Athena, Orestes, Apollo, a representative of the Chorus of Furies). During the presentation, the actors can read from their script.

As a warm-up, you may ask the groups to first capture in a still image the essence of the scene, after having deliberated on its main dramatic event.

Let the groups scatter in the room separately to experiment/improvise with spatial arrangements, set furniture, and audience placement in different parts of the space. In their attempt to come up with compelling ways to integrate elements into their interpretation, participants may use as many props and set pieces in the room as they want. By the end of their brief rehearsal period, each group should be prepared to let everyone know where they are to be seated and assign tasks, if necessary. They may, for example, raise the level of excitement by introducing new parameters (such as giving the audience one or two lines from the text; asking a member of the audience to address one of the characters with a question, forming an actual procession that includes the audience members, etc.). Such elements are bound to heighten the participatory effect of the scene.

When the presentations are over, ask the audience (the other group members) to comment on the affective impact of each act of spectating. When did they feel the theme of justice and the celebration of constitutional rule emerge more powerfully? Did they get alternative glimpses at the essence of the situation every time their participatory function changed? Did they acquire new insights about the world of the play? Were they exposed to different events when asked to perform the Athenian jurors to those they experienced when they became the vicious Furies or when they watched from a safe distance?

Ask each group to describe the manner in which they approached the trial scene. What was the thought behind each placement of the audience?

If time permits, you may wrap-up the exercise by inviting everyone to write down on a piece of paper one sentence that mirrors the play's significance today. These observations can then be read out loud.

Note

1 The term was introduced by American scholar Bonnie Marranca, who described mediaturgy as a methodology of composition and a design of narrative in performance (Marranca 2009).

WORKS CITED

Big Art Group. Web. 28 September 2017. http://bigartgroup.com.

Blast Theory. Web. 20 August 2017. https://www.blasttheory.co.uk/about-us/.

Cardullo, R. J. *Play Analysis. A Casebook on Modern Western Drama.* Rotterdam: Sense Publishers, 2015.

Churchill, Caryl. *Plays: Four (NHB Modern Plays).* London: Nick Hern Books, 2008.

Cohen, Robert and John Harrop. 1974. *Creative Play Direction.* Englewood Cliffs, NJ: Prentice Hall, 1984.

Delgado, Maria M. and Paul Heritage, eds. *In Contact with the Gods? Directors Talk Theatre.* Manchester: Manchester University Press, 1996.

Dietrich, John E. and Ralph W. Duckwall. *Play Direction.* Englewood Cliffs, NJ: Prentice Hall, Inc., 1983 (1953).

Edgar, David. *How Plays Work.* London: Nick Hern Books, 2009.

Gobsquad. Web. 10 September 2017. http://www.gobsquad.com/about-us.

Hutcheon, Linda. *A Theory of Adaptation.* New York: Routledge, 2006.

Icke, Robert. Interviewed by Clapp 2015, *The Guardian,* 23 August 2015. https://www.theguardian.com/stage/2015/aug/23/robert-icke-director-oresteia-1984-interview.

Kerkhoven, Marianne van. "Introduction to 'On Dramaturgy,'" *Theatersthrift* (Brussels: Kaaitheater) No. 5–6, (1994): 8–34.

Mallarmé, Stéphane. *Oeuvres Complètes.* Paris: Pleiade, 1970.

Mamet, David. *True and False. Heresy and Common Sense for the Actor.* New York: Vintage, 1999.

Marranca, Bonnie. "Mediaturgy: A Conversation with Marianne Weems." *International Journal of Arts and Technology* (IJART), Vol. 2, No. 3 (2009): 173–186.

Mitter, Shomit and Maria Shevtsova, eds. *Fifty Key Theatre Directors.* London and New York: Routledge, 2005.

Pfister, Manfred. *The Theory and Analysis of Drama.* Cambridge: Cambridge University Press, 1998.

Stanislavski, Constantin. *An Actor Prepares*. Trans. E. R. Hapgood. London and New York: Routledge, 1989.

States, Bert O. "The Anatomy of Dramatic Character." *Theatre Journal*, Vol. 37, No. 1, "Theory" (March 1985): 86–101.

Stephens, Simon. *Plays 2*. London: Methuen Drama, 2009.

Thomas, James. *Script Analysis for Actors, Directors, and Designers*. Fourth Edition. Burlington and Oxford: Elsevier, Focal Press, 2009.

Trencsenyi, Katalin and Bernadette Cochrane, eds. *New Dramaturgy. International Perspectives on Theory and Practice*. London: Bloomsbury, 2014.

Walsh, Enda. *Ballyturk*. London: Nick Hern Books, 2014.

Chapter 5

Director and Stage

Form

The director balances between the abstract and the concrete first and foremost by visualizing the play and deciding on a concept of staging that can yield a three-dimensional world. Working with design is a struggle to come up with functional and bold solutions to render the visual and the aural environment of the play dynamic and surprising. Solving the form "problem" is no easy task. Even at their most adventurous, forms are assessed against the restrictions imposed by the physical performance space and the production's stylistic and practical requirements. Although in most professional theatres design choices will come at an early stage, usually before rehearsals begin, form will constantly evolve and incorporate rehearsal insights, creative accidents, a better understanding of both text and space.

The semiotician Anne Ubersfeld thinks of staging as a physical application of the setting's metaphoric meaning, which "involves choosing between the different spatial networks, or keeping them together in a relationship of conflict: the text and the staging clarify each other when the point of view is chosen." Such choice depends on "the relation, at the time of the performance, between the staging of the play and the play's contemporary referent and with the code currently in force" (Ubersfeld 1999, 111). Ideally, different approaches to staging and design give you room to explore the flow of the text from the safety of a given form.

Form is what holds the *mise-en-scène* together, being the totality of elements that designate the aesthetic form of performance. Being a combination of the various stylistic principles that communicate the director's vision, it is articulated through set, costume, lighting, and sound design, and often, the presence of technology onstage.

Sometimes, having a conceptual frame predecided earlier on can feel forced, especially to the actors, who commonly like to work organically. It can, however, give enormous freedom to the company. The limitations of a dynamic conceptual frame invite artists to be adventurous with it, create in it, build on it, transcend it.

Set Design

Every aspect of design—set, costume, lighting, or sound—combines art and craft, inspiration and method, imagination and technical expertise. In the past, the creative part of the design process was almost always exclusively attributed to the director, whose vision the designers had to serve and execute technically. This, of course, is no longer the case; designers are no mere facilitators but key interpreters, who work in dialogue with the director.

Modern design began in the early twentieth century with Edward Gordon Craig and Adolphe Appia, both of whom advocated the importance of a "plastic" scenic space, energized by lighting. They opted for simplicity and suggestion, dismissing two-dimensional scenery paintings in favor of architectural elements like platforms and ramps. Space became kinetic and transformational, with high emotional power, an instrumental player in performance. Already in 1820, the introduction of gas lighting had been a breakthrough in stagecraft, supporting various aesthetic possibilities with regards to creating atmosphere and intensity. Craig's and Appia's theories greatly influenced contemporary set and lighting design. Today, aesthetic stylization is facilitated by the resourceful development of flexible, architectural, energetic spaces, also allowing the rhythm of lighting to infiltrate performance. In fact, scenography and lighting are constitutive aspects of a stage *écriture*, where "the painterly and sculptural qualities of performance are stressed, transforming this theatre into a spatially dominated one activated by sense impressions, as opposed to a time-dominated one ruled by linear narrative" (Marranca 1977, xii). Back in 1941, American set designer Robert Edmund Jones argued that the designing of stage scenery was "not the problem of an architect or a painter or a sculptor or even a musician, but of a poet" (2004, 22–23).

According to Pamela Howard's concise definition, scenography (or else, set design) is "the seamless synthesis of space, text, research, art, actors, directors, and spectators that contributes to an original creation" (Howard 2001, postscript). At the onset of a new project, directors and their designers will work together to turn a given space into a familiar place for the actors and a home for the characters. As Howard argues, understanding scenography starts with understanding the potential of the empty performance space. It then considers the spoken word, text, or music that transforms an empty space into an auditorium (xix). A dynamic space—be it realistic/mimetic, symbolic/metaphoric, or abstract/poetic—creates expectations of surprising action and reinvents established staging conventions, as in fact does the innovative use of lighting, costumes, and props.

In the last few decades of the twentieth century, a unified scenographic concept came to replace bulky scene-per-scene sets that were meant to introduce a different design environment to match the variety of settings described in the text. This economy in design has contributed to a more functional use of space and taken attention away from the logistics of moving pieces of scenery around and carrying out elaborate transitions. Constitutional to sensory impact, design not only resolves complex issues of staging but also releases textual meaning and opens up paths for the director and the actors to further explore both the operative and the emotive environment of the play. After their selection, objects and images are "translated into moments of significance" (McKinney and Butterworth 2009, 191). Being more than an accurate 3D and sequential description of the geographical locations indicated in the text, scenography frames the action according to decisions that express a specific interpretation of temporality and locality, and reveals information about the season, time of the day, the passage of time, and the nature of people's attitudes.

> Space is established in pointers of geographical location and specific setting details (interior and exterior), either explicit (stated in the stage directions) or implicit (embedded in the dialogue). Because set design is no mere physicalization of *didascaliae* referencing location, it expands beyond architecture to encompass the mental and psychological event that the director wishes the audience to experience. An evocative design is suggestive and metaphoric, arousing memories as well as new provocations in the spectators' mind, all the while retaining the necessary level of abstraction, a valuable principle in any work of art. It, is functional and poetic, consistent but also surprising, producing aesthetic pleasure and visceral access to the life of the text.

Finally, design is a major anchor of context. We have already explained the function of metaphor in performance. Because of their complexity, scenographic metaphors are challenging, requiring more audience time to be processed fully. Not rarely, anachronisms support the playful interaction of the original text with the text of the *mise-en-scène*. In productions set in a period removed from the present, intelligent design imparts point of view and gives prominence to the original play's cultural coordinates. By properly updating the setting, an abstract or an eclectic design that fuses elements from different historical periods can effectively reenergize centuries-old texts.

Director-Designer Collaboration

The relationship with the designer is perhaps the most creative and exciting among all the artistic relationships to which directors commit. In the history of theatre, visionary dialogues and sustained aesthetic bonds between the two have left a lasting mark on many productions. Collaborations such as the ones between Konstantin Stanislavski and Viktor Simov, Giorgio Strehler and Luciano Damiani, Thomas Ostermeier and Jan Pappelbaum, or Ivo van Hove and Jan Versweyveld have repeatedly validated the inseparable, vital connection of scenography with the art of directing. Howard understands this collaboration as a meeting of a literary and a spatial imagination, whereby the set designer is a "director of space, a visual director," no longer a "decorator of directorial concepts," but "an architect of the imagination" (in Oddey and White 2006, 28, 30).

The designer's work process is remarkably similar to that of the director, as it evolves from an intuitive response to the text and a detailed analysis of its spatial parameters to an actual implementation of the design concept. Once again, design starts with a "creative reading," is supported by free drawings and collages of the designer's first responses, proceeds to research and, is finally delivered in a finished model of the set. If anything, both directors and designers must be familiar with every nook and cranny of the script, since it is primarily in the text that the energy of the space and possible staging configurations will be revealed. After you have sufficiently explained your vision and described your idea of the design concept in broad terms, inevitably you will need to surrender to the expertise of the scenographer, who is technically equipped to foresee potential risks and offer alternatives. For that, it is necessary to develop a shared visual vocabulary. In actual practice

> The stage designer directs options for movement by providing levels, entrances, physical obstacles and motivational objectives for actors. Directors exploit these options to design and create compositions which reveal the conflicts and action of the play. Designers provide textures, colors and volumes, line, highlight, shadow and contrast to stimulate the senses of actors and audiences in kinaesthetic and visual ways. Directors integrate actors into and out of the environments created by designers.
>
> (Erven in White 2009, 24)

In the director-designer collaboration, directors gradually learn to think like a designer, becoming familiar with principal design elements such as line, proportion, angle, and shape. Such knowledge will lead to a more informed understanding of the complexity of scenography and the demands that specific spaces posit on the production concept. Reversely, designers become versed in fundamental directing concepts, such as blocking and composition. After all, every designer is a director of sorts, who works from freedom to technique, from an instinctual response to solid production structures.

Commitment, trust, and flexibility are quintessential elements of collaboration. New possibilities may show only when you are prepared to see things afresh. Try to communicate your ideas with clarity from the beginning, but also be willing to revise them according to valuable designer feedback. Keeping an open mind can lead to mutually satisfying metaphors and, in turn, a well-conceived, well-crafted design can solve movement issues and so make your job a lot easier. Where honesty and listening are present, design challenges will be addressed faster and more proficiently. In this sense, it may be worth repeating that set designers are not designated "executioners" of a vague scenographic concept. They, too, invest in the text, ask valid dramaturgical questions, and calibrate point of view. Adapting to the changed circumstances of the design means that, as rehearsals develop, the set can be adjusted to eliminate impractical staging choices and accommodate added functions and revised blocking that could not have been predicted originally.

Be prepared to reexamine your original concept if the designer comes up with a new intriguing thought. Ideas are always developing, and any experienced director knows how to trust changes that seem necessary, even if it means having to make radical adjustments and toss earlier decisions. In the process of design, rigidity is an enemy.

How Set Design Evolves

In general, the stylistic and practical demands of each scene are studied thoroughly in a series of director-designer meetings before the designer hands over to the director the final 3D model of the set design.

Important things to consider are the historical context in which the play is set originally or to which the action is transferred by an act of updating. Also, the preferred style of the production and the transitions from one location to the next, including movement from the outdoors to the indoors and vice versa. Similarly, the blocking of the actors and any unusual movement, such as people or objects hanging from the ceiling, trapdoors opening, water onstage, snow falling, etc., but also sightlines, exact entrances and exits, and, finally, moments of dramatic focus. Other considerations include areas of danger and tension and possible sources of scenographic surprise. You must also take into account how private or public a scene is and the levels of formality embedded in each setting.

In most professional productions, a while before the actors come into the picture, you can expect the set designer to deliver a ground plan of the design to scale; drawings of the set; and finally, a model. The design operation is set in motion with visual hints and tentative suggestions, often in the form of preliminary sketches depicting potentially weighty design moments in the performance. Early impressions are preliminary instigations to further detailed work and useful for eliciting spontaneous responses. Significantly, having your designers put down in drawing their uncensored ideas is a way of conceding creative ownership of the text. After a round of conversations concerning your overall concept, where costume and lighting designers are also present, you can review different lists of textual information directly or indirectly related to issues of space. These typically include stage directions or dialogue parts with clues about geographical location, season, time of the day, the weather conditions, and architectural details of interiors, furniture, and props. With the directorial concept adequately discussed, a creative phase of preparation follows course. Period and other research feeds your imagination, zooming into the characters' everyday reality, with all its minute routines.

> Compelling designs combine two seemingly conflicting dimensions: theatre being an art form, it encourages the expansion into the parabolic, the universal, and the larger-than-life. At the same time, a play is always rooted in a particular environment, being often a critique of the characters' cultural life.

Storyboarding the script, which puts design ideas into preliminary visual form, comes next. The storyboard takes into account every set or costume item onstage, including what needs to be shifted during transitions. Designers produce drawings that follow a rough staging pictorially and scene-by-scene (or key scene-by-key scene); the entire story is visually transcribed into an imagistic score, illustrating on paper the principal events of crucial dramatic moments. When enough research and designer homework has been gathered, a picture gallery of the accumulated material in the space can serve as a helpful visual reference and a constant reminder to the company of the new habitat they will be sharing for the next few weeks or months.

In the end, what determines the movement of the design, its secrets, and surprises, is rehearsal work. The ideas that evolve within a studio context are inevitably exposed to the challenges introduced by the actors, who carry in them strong interpretative acumen. In other words, the actual design that was first presented in the scale model can only come alive in the performers' presence. This makes it imperative that the set, which is ordinarily agreed on before rehearsals begin, is flexible enough to facilitate any adjustments that become necessary as soon as the actors start to interact with it. Having said that, although the final physical set will not be realized and delivered until just days before tech week, it is essential to work with some of its core elements (this also applies to costumes and props), even if they are only reproductions of the final set pieces. This will give performers the chance to become familiar as early as possible with the material world of the production and address problems that may potentially surface with regards to its use. Guide your actors through every corner of the set, explaining how it functions, whether it changes, and if it holds any traps or surprises, including tricky sightlines.

Costumes and Lighting

Costume Design

A theatrical costume is the characters' most private home, releasing their personality. It is not just daily wear, but a projection of attitude, and a visual communication of a whole time period. The same way that whatever we put onstage is necessarily compressed, being a statement of several things, costumes are primarily distillations of the director's interpretation of character, conveying different kinds of information: social and economic background and class, style, taste, and mood of the moment. They also sculpt and paint space. Integrated into or set against the scenery, they shape visual patterns and add color. What is more, they can provide emphasis, isolating one character while highlighting another, and let performers embody multiple roles. They also act as sophisticated personality or cultural signifiers, imparting specific characteristics, which are stated or implied. Contributing to the play's atmosphere, they can truly influence the audience's sensory involvement.

Costume design supports character interpretation. It is a carrier of identity, but also, a major signifying system of the verbal text, coded with historical, sociological, status, gender, and psychological significance.

How does a theatre costume come to life? Lengthy, comprehensive research and careful observation of textual clues before and during rehearsals help designate the characters' identity and their surroundings. Quite akin to the development of the set, costume design evolves from drawings of initial ideas—this time, about character. As conversations between director and designer progress, the images will get more elaborate, featuring detail and texture. Fabric swaps are also brought in to bridge the gap between the original phase of conceptualization and the concrete execution of costumes. Because costumes can either liberate or confine characters and performers, it is advisable that you and your designer pay attention to the actors' opinions about how comfortable or uncomfortable they may feel in them. In fact, you need to make sure that actors have enough time to rehearse with their costumes (or in the very least with some basic accessories) to be better prepared to handle potential mishaps in performance. Knowing their costumes is for them a way of feeling good in their character skin.

Lighting Design

On the whole, modern theatre design is far from being concerned to serve an exclusively utilitarian purpose. Instead, it often features unconventional configurations that are predominantly metaphoric. Theorized by Edward Gordon Craig and Adolphe Appia, set and lighting design became inspirational arts on their own, as early as the beginnings of the twentieth century. For Appia, mobile, interpretive lighting consolidated setting, action, and actors into an inspired whole. Notably, it was also seen as drama's visual counterpart to music, following language's internal rhythmic movement. Today, lighting is "no longer about unity but about transition" (Aronson 2008, 35), and, in that sense, "what we don't see becomes as important as what we do see" (36).

Lighting reveals, describes, clarifies, focuses, and connects. It manipulates location, temporality, and distance, introduces geography, weather conditions, and season. It also evokes feelings, induces atmosphere, uncovers possible conflict, and intensifies charged moments of the action.

The different properties and functions of lighting instruments are the subject of the art and science of lighting design and will not be discussed here. Although, strictly speaking, few directors are technical experts on lighting and usually rely on a more general vocabulary to communicate with their designers, a practical understanding of basic principles of lighting design always proves helpful. Even a beginner director will know, for example, that spotlights focus the audience's attention on a particular character or place onstage. Or, that follow spots are habitually used in musicals or big-scale commercial productions, front lights are common in realistic drama, backlights create the illusion of depth, and side lights accentuate the performer's body and are particularly useful in dance.

Lighting designers are present in the director's initial production meetings with the set and costume designers, and often the producer, too. Alongside discussing functionality and budget, those meetings determine the production's style, and bring to the table different options for color, line, and shape. When the concept of the set and the costumes is settled, you will work with the lighting designer more closely, especially as tech week approaches. Over the course of rehearsals, you may have one or two more targeted individual meetings, before he or she hands in the lighting plot, that is, the technical sheet that specifies the exact position of the lighting instruments onstage and is the basis for examining lighting choices for different moments in performance.

For collaboration to feel constructive, it helps to remind yourself that lighting designers work under a lot of pressure, being responsible for the bulk of the work during tech week. This involves long and exhausting cue-to-cue sessions, where lighting design is practically implemented, technical run-throughs, where problems are being addressed, and dress rehearsals, after which only slight adjustments to lighting are allowed. In point of fact, during tech, besides deciding where in performance the lighting shifts and preparing the corresponding cue sheet with the designer and the SM, your chief responsibility is to remain calm and keep the company's spirit high. For this brief, stressful period, you will inevitably share with your lighting designer a great part of your responsibilities as the show's principal orchestrator.

Composition

No performance exists in a vacuum, not least those taking place on an empty stage. Dramatic situation is organized and brought to life through scenography as well as the placement of animate and inanimate elements in various changing relationships to each other. The static arrangement of performers onstage, together in groups or separated by physical distance, is called composition. Such placement can induce meaningful pictures, which express weighty moments of action in aesthetically fulfilling ways. Composition tells the story of the play with no words or movement, framing each scene by highlighting cardinal dramatic events visually. The way the actors' bodies are set against each other will tell a different story each time. In this respect, every ground plan—a bird's-eye view of the stage, usually a scale drawing of the theatre space containing all the scenery items—will suggest configurations that may signify completely different things through emphasis or contrast.

Unusual compositions delight audiences. They focus attention on the important moments and subtly hint at character relationships. Always try to outsmart the dangers of prosaic, all-too-familiar forms, manipulating the uncomfortable space and distance afforded by an out-of-scale, slightly off-angle perspective or an unexpected juxtaposition of performers and set. Understanding the function of composition is a valuable directorial skill. Develop it further by observing people's physical behavior and contemplating works of art.

Picturization

While composition is a still-shot image of a stage event, picturization is the transition from one composition to the next, animated by the actors' movement, gestures, and stage business. As an operation that activates the image created by the arrangement of bodies onstage, it can be variously described as a physicalization of a narrative line, an actioned story, or a kinetic fulfillment of composition. In another definition, it is the "storytelling by a group of people," brought about by "the combined use of composition (the arrangement of the group), gesture (the individual moving within his own sphere), and improvisation with properties (objects added to composition and gesture) for the specific purpose of animating the dramatic action" (Hodge 1994, 135). All in all, picturization is the visual activity that mobilizes and unifies a set of compositions.

Focus

Directorial emphasis has been briefly discussed earlier on in the book, with reference to how point of view organizes moments in the play that the director considers significant. Visual emphasis, in particular, is embedded into composition and picturization. By controlling the position or movement of an actor, a scenographic element or a prop, a director can achieve different depths or levels of stage focus. In fact, focus suggests that something is visibly pronounced in relation to the element/s around it, whether that concerns the actor/character, a specific area of the stage or a piece of scenery. In general, the closer an actor is to the audience or the more centrally placed, the stronger the focus he or she will attract.

Focus is also obtained by means of distance among the performers. Above all, the act of physically separating one actor from another or from the group—by space or lighting—establishes contrast, which is an integral element of stage emphasis. Focus also goes to the speaking actor in a group of silent performers, an actor who moves when everyone else is still or an actor who breaks out of a pattern followed by the rest. The way you implement and shift stage dynamics significantly affects the performer's spatial relationship to the audience, enhancing its experience and quality of attention. In fact, the use of proxemics should be in every director's toolkit.

Composition and blocking also reinforce character status. Just as there are strong and weak areas onstage, there are also strong and weak positions for achieving spatial focus, an understanding that can help when you experiment with relationship dynamics. Naturally, stage positions have their own unique life: an actor positioned at the center of the stage facing the audience full front will inevitably attract more attention and obtain higher status than the one facing upstage; similarly, an actor standing is more powerful than one sitting, and so forth.

Stage Areas, Planes, Levels, Angles

Similarly, the bold exploitation of stage areas, planes, levels, and angles is bound to produce a sense of adventure in performance. As demonstrated, playing with space also means experimenting with actor placement to furnish an assortment of compositions, each influencing visual perception differently. Stage areas and levels (actors standing, stooping, sitting), horizontal locations (placement along the width of the stage), and planes (designating depth on the proscenium stage) communicate additional information about characters and their rapport.

Typically strong compositions include triangles, diagonals, extreme distance or proximity, dense and crowded spaces, and performer isolation. Contrary, for instance, to the placement of figures or objects parallel to the proscenium, diagonal lines convey the passage of time and tend to be used in psychologically loaded scenes to establish danger or tension. Similarly, the cross from upstage to downstage indicates deliberation and choice, whereas the upstage area is fraught with associations of the characters' past, and often bears an aura of mystery. Levels and the vertical visuality of raked floors, ramps, ladders, and scaffolds give variety and depth of focus, expanding the playing area and propagating infinite combinations of movement.

Blocking

Staging is the careful coordination of the principal aspects of design (set, costume, lighting, video, and sound) to set up a stylistically unified environment. Blocking, on the other hand, concerns the movement of the actors onstage. It is the detailed physicalization of a series of actions that allows director and actor to animate the world of the play, clarify motivations, and instigate emotive progress. For the actor to be visible at all times, blocking is applied to every unit of every scene, but as a rule, that comes after the director has envisioned the rhythm and shape of movement for the entire performance. As one would expect, blocking ideas begin to form concurrently to reading, if only because visualization is an intrinsic aspect of text analysis. In fact, "every reading of the theatre text imposes choices of spatial structuring, as soon as one has to decide *who* is speaking and according to what proxemic relationships" (Pavis 1993, 156, original emphasis).

As a director blocking the play, you will need to take into account the structural anchors of each scene, the moment of climax as well as the principal stage areas, the alternation between slow and fast pace and the actors' entrances and exits. Quite often, you can pre-block different sequences, creating a general floor pattern for every actor's movement, with the understanding that during run-throughs, you will probably need to make adjustments and add more detail to improve moments in the action that may feel vague or general.

Stage traffic is not something that can be predetermined on paper. All pre-blocking decisions should be considered provisional until they are evaluated empirically in the rehearsal room. No matter how much thought you have put into planning the blocking early on, you can only finalize the exact movement after several days or weeks of sorting things out physically with the actors. As the blocking phase gradually blends into run-throughs, you can check what works and what doesn't, using the expert advice of your set designer, to fine-tune elements that still need attention. For focus and variety in the blocking, it is advisable to watch for those particular moments in the play that introduce new information and relationship dynamics.

Atmosphere and Mood

Movement, the physical change of the characters across the space of the stage, will be addressed separately in the final chapter of the book, which concerns the director's work with the actor. The analysis of visual form could only conclude with stressing the importance of atmosphere and mood in creating sensory impact. While they are both influenced by the stimulating synergies of set, costume, and lighting design, the distinction between them is rather ambiguous. Mood usually describes the feeling that emanates from a character or a group of characters together, whereas atmosphere is the broader emotive ambience of a scene or a play, combining mood, imagery, language, and patterns of rhythm. As they are received through neurological channels, the two affect our perception beyond logical reasoning, originating sentiments of happiness or sorrow, of fear, relief, and tranquility; generally, such affective qualities can make the world of the play *feel* light and fast pacing, cold and hostile, mysterious or domestic. Evidently, the more abrupt and surprising the shifts in mood are, the more powerful their effect is on the audience.

As it cultivates visceral sensation through colors, shapes, and symbols, scenography can be particularly suggestive of atmosphere and mood. Lighting, on the other hand, further to establishing atmosphere, can change the emotional conditions of each scene to match the rhythm of storytelling; producing feelings radically or subtly, it often robs us of the habit of logically processing polysemous lines of narrative. Actors, too, sustain or upset existing moods by sheer quality of their physical life, which will always convey the character's attitude "in the moment." Finally, blocking also creates mood, externalizing inner motivations. For instance, conflict can be expressed using extreme distance, while feelings of despair and sadness are usually a matter of controlling the timing of a physical response.

> Atmosphere and mood concern the ways in which a director arranges the emotional cadences of the text, using forms of staging that enhance affective properties in the context of performance.

WORKBOOK 5.1

Practice 1. Composition and Focus

The following exercises suggest different ways of building a story visually. They hint at the countless possibilities of a given theatre space and of the different means of achieving focus and status through composition. They also point to ways of controlling the dynamics of planes and levels. Because focus is an aspect of composition that draws the audience's attention to where it "should" be looking, it may be useful to follow up the exercises with a feedback session and get the actors to openly discuss how practical or effective a particular actor placement was.

Activity 1. Configuring Space

In your play of choice, decide on three spatial configurations for the same scene. Choose contrast between interior/exterior, upstage/downstage, and crowded/uncongested playing areas.

- How much of the story can we gather merely by watching?
- Do you notice any differences in the way the story is told?
- In what ways, if any, are the dynamics of character relationships affected?

Activity 2. Gallery Visit

Take your group of actors on a field trip to a museum or an art gallery. Visit different sections and rooms, enjoying the work of artists from different periods of time. The medieval Flemish paintings, as well as the Italian Renaissance masters, are particularly fitting for a study of composition. An excellent case in point would be Hieronymus Bosch's three-paneled work *The Garden of Earthly Delights* (1490–1500), Peter Bruegel the Elder's *Peasant Dance* (1586), and Michelangelo's famous fresco *Creation of Adam* in the Vatican Sistine Chapel's ceiling (1508–1512).

- Choose a painting from each section and thoroughly examine its main compositional principles. Have the group decide what the story in each picture is and identify its focal point.
- On which element or figure does the weight of the painting fall?
- What are the strengths and weaknesses of the composition?
- What is the relationship of the figures to the viewer?
- What is the overall mood of each composition?
- After you return to the rehearsal studio, the actors can work in groups to stage still images inspired by one of these compositions and then give a title to each.

Activity 3. Stage Placement and Focus 1

In *Death of a Salesman*, stage the opening scene between Willy and Linda, focusing alternately on each of the two characters, as they set up the emotional tone of the play. Experiment with different placements onstage (Center Stage [CS], Stage Left [SL], Stage Right [SR], downstage and upstage), and exploit the physical distance between the performers and their closeness to the audience to change their status and influence the direction toward which their relationships develop.

Activity 4. Stage Placement and Focus 2

With your group of actors look into ways of achieving stage emphasis and status, and also change the compositional make-up of the scene across five frames. Start with three performers, and then increase the number to six.

- Give each actor a different position onstage and decide on your point of focus, using stage positions and proxemics.
- Choose the actor/actors who are going to receive emphasis at all times. Think of different ways to make them more visible than the others (have them standing when everyone else is sitting, remaining center stage, facing the audience directly when everyone else is facing away, being physically isolated from the rest of the group, etc.).
- What kind of effect is achieved in each of your compositions?
- Once your compositions are arranged, add variation. You may select a character who seems emotionally closer to your protagonist and modify the composition accordingly. Observe how the balance of the scene tips with this addition.

Activity 5. Stage Placement and Focus 3

Place four actors onstage, asking them to assume any position in a designated playing area.

Have them identify a potential character-magnet and make their relationship to him or her known by accordingly changing their physical position in relation to the character in question. They must be able to switch compositionally to convey emotions of attraction, enmity, apathy, etc.

Activity 6. Ground Plan and Point of View

In your play of choice, concentrate on two principal scenes and draft a ground plan for the spatial arrangements you envision. List two essential features of the ground plan, such as an existing staircase or a large piece of furniture.

Change the ground plan by playing with the dimensions, angle of walls, and placement of objects to offer an alternative perspective to the play. You may want to add levels, furniture, or stairs.

Keep revising your ground plan to expand the range of compositional and blocking possibilities.

From each different ground plan what can you deduce about the use of space, the kind of relationships it encourages, the movement that could materialize in it, and the overall spatial logic?

Activity 7. Photographic Composition

As a group exercise, have your actors bring in web photos, newspaper clips, theatre programs and posters of their favorite productions, and ask them to comment on exciting compositional moments in performance, as depicted in the images.

Decide on the most compelling features of the compositions and discuss how dynamically they evolved onstage.

Discover which character or characters are in focus and what their relationship to the other characters onstage is.

Identify the central conflict of each composition and, in particular, the nature of the conflict and the characters it primarily affects.

Practice 2. Picturization and Blocking

The following activities also intend to have the group work with principles of spatial structuration. They are primarily geared toward picturization and blocking, that is, the manner in which the position of one actor (or a group of actors) to another and to the audience can influence storytelling.

Activity I. Blocking the Scene

Block the final scene (Scene 11) of *A Streetcar Named Desire*, in which Blanche is being led out of the Kowalski household and onto a psychiatric ward.

- Create a ground plan for the scene and build your series of compositions carefully, incorporating a diverse use of levels, plane areas, and angles.

- There are several characters present onstage. How are you going to group them? Rethink obvious configurations (such as having Eunice and Stella be physically close to Blanche) in favor of more daring choices (e.g., Stanley and his buddies involving Stella or the Matron in their game of cards).
- If the focus is on Blanche, where are you going to place her onstage? What is her relationship to the audience going to be?
- Experiment profusely, and think whether an unorthodox, unpredictable moment of staging could better illuminate the scene or would, reversely, destabilize your point of view. Carefully consider which ground plan would better serve your interpretation of the scene and the play as a whole.

Activity 2. Picturization

Build a story in pictures, using two actors and two chairs. Use composition to picturize the following familiar situations:

- A family quarrel
- A love confession
- A job interview
- A doctor-patient consultation, with the breaking of bad news
- A teacher-pupil interaction, where the former reprimands the latter for inappropriate behavior
- Two old friends reuniting after a very long time
- Two friends gossiping in a coffee shop

Activity 3. Transforming the Space

In a classical play of choice, provide different points of view by alternately applying the following three different styles of design on a pivotal scene:

- Realistic-Period
- Symbolist-Abstract
- Eclectic

Shakespeare's plays are a good fit here, as they can be freely adapted and updated, and still retain their meaning and poetry.

Sound and Technology

Sound

Mise-en-Sound

Sound relays the aural interpretation of the play. A compelling aspect of performance, it imparts information and is also one of the most intuitive ways for building mood and raising the production's emotional stakes. Sound designers synthesize instances of *mise-en-sound* by variously applying original or existing music, sound effects, or acoustic ambiance on sound environments that are often texts in themselves. Commenting on the function of sound design in contemporary theatre, Peter Sellars explains that we are "beyond the era of sound 'effects'":

> Sound is no longer an effect, an extra, a garni supplied from time to time to mask a scene change or ease a transition. We are beyond the era of door buzzers and thunderclaps. Or rather, door buzzers and thunderclaps are no longer isolated effects, but part of a total program of sound that speaks to theater as ontology. Sound is the holistic process and program that binds our multifarious experience of the world. Sound is our own inner continuity track. It is also our primary outward gesture to the world, our first and best chance to communicate with others, to become part of a larger rhythm.
>
> (Sellars in Kay and LeBrecht, 2009, ix)

One need only recall Simon McBurney's *The Encounter* (2015) to acknowledge that the admission of innovative sound technology into the theatre has amplified and deepened audience perception. Inspired by Petru Popescu's book *Amazon Beaming*, McBurney's solo piece tells the story of a National Geographic photographer, Loren McIntyre, who in 1969 journeyed through the Amazon, an encounter that brought the "limits of human consciousness into startling focus" (http://www.complicite.org/productions/theencounter). At the beginning of the show, the audience is asked to wear headphones of 3D technology, which will be kept on the entire time. As a result, every sound the protagonist is experiencing during his fascinating voyage becomes part of our acoustic awareness. We hear his live voice but are also occasionally startled by resonant prerecorded sounds, such as his young daughter's pleas to be told a bedtime story and whose apparent physical placement behind our backs renders us silent but involved witnesses to the events that unfold thereafter. McBurney's binaural audio, in all its deceptive, shocking proximity, encourages the spectator's empathy with McIntyre's ordeals, as the journalist follows the members of an Amazon tribe through a wilderness haunted by sounds.

Aural imagination could be described as the capacity to conceive of theme, mood, and narrative line in sonic terms. Deena Kay and James LeBrecht call this process of "imagining sound in space, over time" "auralizing" (Kay and LeBrecht 2009, 13). In fact, similarly to how a set designer visualizes the world of the play, a sound designer *auralizes* it.

The Process

Working with sound always starts with the text and the auditory clues it contains. Here too, the stage directions are the director's and the sound designer's most important source, but leads are often provided in the dialogue. The given circumstances of location, historical period, season, and time of the day relate to specific settings, actions, and moods, which, in turn, convey explicit or implicit suggestions of sound and music. Make a note of all the sound cues already indicated in the script, irrespective of whether or how you are going to use them.

In your collaboration with the designer, you set things in motion by discussing the general feel of the play and what you want to evoke through sound and music. What follows is a detailed inventory of each sound, special effect, or transition music meant to bring the play alive acoustically—you can first listen to all the sounds in the text and gradually review any additional sounds you wish to include in performance. When the sound designer is also a composer, original musical scores can also be requested. A realistic play will require realistic sound cues, dependent on the accurate reproduction of existing, recognizable sounds. An expressionistic piece can benefit significantly from a jarring sound score or unusual discords. Specific genres, such as musicals, are a category of their own. (Musical) directors will, by and large, treat the composer as a writer and the collaboration with the sound designer will be of a more technical nature.

> In thinking about sound, fundamental principles of design also apply, as creating sound for the theatre generally follows the course of scenography and costumes. Each play dictates its unique musical treatment, according to setting, content, and style, and as a result, sound design will be eclectic or period specific, realistic or abstract, baroque or minimalist.

Both style and concept of design, settled early on, will lead to specific aesthetic and technical choices. This is why you and your designer need to develop a mutually convenient vocabulary—sounds, for example, can be described as harsh, soft, mellow, threatening, or soothing.

Undoubtedly, the more precise the adjectives, the easier it will be for the sound designer to work with amorphous ideas. Moreover, where a particular musical piece is indicated, you also need to consider its place and function in the play carefully before deciding what to do with it. Try also to decide on any special sounds early enough, to give your designer enough time to weigh various technical possibilities and do the necessary research, starting from more general parameters, such as, for example, location and time. In the meantime, rough musical and sound ideas can be brought in for you, piece by piece, to listen to and select from.

For a variety of reasons, including cost, level of difficulty, lack of rehearsal time, or lack of resources, you may have the sound prerecorded and played out from the theatre machinery. Other times, you can use live music and on-stage effects, while a mixture of the two is also possible. The on-stage functions of sounds are also significant: some will be heard by the characters onstage (this is especially true of realistic effects, such as thunder, a knock on the door, a telephone ringing), whereas others will be reserved for emphasis and mood—heard by the audience but "unheard" by the characters. Often, a background soundscape can cover an entire scene, or even the entire play, providing an acoustic environment. Sometimes, preshow music introduces the spectator into the prevailing mood of the opening moments. In addition, sound is employed structurally to mark the change between scenes, the beginning of the show or the curtain call, and facilitate the passing from one location to the next. On the whole, music is an excellent means of covering scene transitions that involve cumbersome set changes and pieces of furniture being moved around. Besides, sound can also be used ironically, to startling effect, as a psychological counterpoint to what is taking place onstage. In this regard, contrast generated musically is particularly compelling, juxtaposing as it does the actual dramatic and emotional significance of a sound against the assumed content of the scene.

Finally, by repeating itself at crucial moments in performance, sound delivers patterns that bear thematic significance, boost storytelling, and provide due emphasis. Typically, patterns are formed when the audience comes to associate specific sounds with specific actions, themes, attitudes, and even characters. Any change in the established sound pattern, no matter how minuscule, will inevitably suggest a change of intention or action. This is why negotiating sound patterns requires a high discipline of thought and logic, as well as imagination. Patterns that are repeated with consistency as affective anchors in certain parts of the performance can support narrative intensity and focus. In reality, an entire offstage reality can be developed from sound, and this is why it always helps to have frequent conversations with your designer, who will probably introduce you to a much fuller range of options than those you may think possible.

Collaboration

Sound technology is advancing so fast that it is virtually impossible for the average director to keep track of the acoustic possibilities available through updated sophisticated computer software and playback systems. Thankfully, rendering an initial impulse into resonant sound is the job of the sound designer, and, as a result, good listening and an open mind can work miracles in the director-designer relationship. They are particularly valuable, given that our culture is mostly visual and it is common for many directors not to be as knowledgeable or articulate about music or sound as they are about other aspects of staging. The abstract nature of music sometimes makes it challenging to express sound ideas with clarity and detail. Quite probably, the majority of directors are less trained to recognize and appreciate sound than to read and reorder images—most people's perception tends to be image-related. This is when the sound designer steps in to discuss more general notions of design, such as feel, depth, intensity, and mood. In the end, if an idea fails to be put across through description, surely you and your designer can share works from a particular musical period and style or by specific composers, as a common point of reference.

Rehearsing with Sound

Since sounds are charged with psychological content, having a reasonably clear idea of what you want to communicate will bring symmetry, consistency and a sense of totality to performance, and give time to the designer to work independently and without too much pressure. After the first couple of director-designer meetings, the approximate length of each sound, as well as the levels of closure (finality) or open-endedness of each scene will also be settled. That said, most of the times, the sound score is modified or enriched *as* the production concept evolves and staging becomes more detailed. When the score is finalized, the exact timing and positioning of the cues follows course, so that, ideally, everything feels relatively in place by the first run-through. Sound levels are determined during tech, but you should be aware of the existing sound sources in the theatre space, before then.

For obvious reasons, actors are anxious to know their sound cues, especially if they are in dialogue with them, responding to or even triggering the sound. In fact, some actors find it difficult and distracting to work with music or sound, unable to either "ignore" it or play with it, as the case may be, especially when they must speak "against it." For this reason, amply rehearse with sound before getting to tech week, to relieve such anxieties and prevent, as much as you can, smaller or bigger misfortunes in performance.

Sound is there to help, rather than hinder the actor's work. Sound cues can be invaluable acting tools, signaling transitions in pregnant dramatic moments and marking different acting units or beats. In this sense, the earlier sound is introduced into rehearsal, the better.

Literalness, Again

Being literal with sound is as big a cardinal sin as is being overly explicit and descriptive with scenography. Applying authentic sound effects in a realistic play is legitimate and necessary; saturating the emotive texture of a scene with heavy-handed musical sequences, no matter how sensational, can accelerate character and action development to such degree that the small, imperceptible psychological steps toward dramaturgical completion may be overlooked on the way. In the end, sound design should never impose itself on the play or outshine the performer. Literalness, the usual suspect we have had to identify time and again, keeps creeping its ugly face in every aspect of directing, not least in the aural. Busy effects tend to diffuse moments of real dramatic significance. A musical score can be overpowering, relying on sentimentalism, and resisting the gradual, slow pleasure of building the feeling of a scene from within. Sometimes, insecurity will have directors entrust the entire storytelling to the associative powers of music and songs. But even if such easy reference could conceivably work momentarily, its impact would only last this long. Ultimately, music/sound and text must work together, with and besides the performer. Balance and—not surprisingly—meaningfulness are once again essential *desiderata*.

WORKBOOK 5.2

Practice I. Becoming Sound Literate

To engage more fully with sound design, you should start thinking about how sound can be used to convey information and produce sensory effect in performance. The following exercises may feel rudimentary but suggest different ways of using sound as an interpretative tool.

Activity I. Hear the Room

It usually takes time and effort to start thinking aurally, since we are primarily visually trained. As an exercise, you can simply have your group close their eyes and try to identify the sounds in the room, isolating the ones that are closer to them from those in the distance.

Activity 2. Sound Detectives

In your free time, record different "sound instances," excluding any dialogue, and play them out to your actors, asking them to guess the source of origin. Present the group with different sound-scapes bearing various gradations of difficulty. For example, you can start with something simple, as is a train approaching an underground platform, pouring wine into a glass, doing the dishes and putting the plates down to dry, typing or reversing the car. You could then move to more sophisticated *sound scenes*, such as beating the eggs for an omelet, sweeping dried leaves in the yard, making the bed, and so forth.

Practice 2. Music and Sound

As a director operating within tight schedules, you rarely have the opportunity to work exclusively or even improvise with sound. The following exercises are experiments that illustrate how sound can be a text in itself, propelling the story forward, at least on an emotional level. They also put into practice the director's auralizing process and bridge the art of directing with that of sound design.

Activity 1. Sounding It Up

Choose a short scene from your play of choice, divest it of all dialogue and try to stage it moment-to-moment, using only music and sound. Think of what you want to achieve in each unit in terms of rhythm, emotion, intensity, dramatic tension, and mood.

Activity 2. Sound Emotions

Choose one musical piece and one sound to express a specific psychological state (e.g., sadness, anger, tenderness, fear, etc.).

Think of a play that evokes these emotions, and try to match dialogue with sound and music.

What do the sound or the music add to our sensory appreciation of the play? Do they overpower the dialogue in any way?

Activity 3. Preparing a Sound Score

In the stage directions of *A Streetcar Named Desire*, the playwright indicates a range of existing musical pieces, as well as sound cues for specific parts of the play.

- While reading the play, make a list of all the sound/musical cues provided by the text: Work as in the following example:
  - Opening scene: the music of Negro entertainers at a barroom around the corner/the blue piano/voices of people on the street can be heard overlapping/A cat screeches/The music of the blue piano grows louder/ The sound of men's voices is heard/A cat screeches near the window/The music of the polka rises up, faint in the distance.
  - Scene 2: leaving the door open on the perpetual blue piano around the corner/The (blue piano sounds louder).
  - Scene 3: Blanche rises and crosses leisurely to a small white radio and turns it on/Rhumba music comes over the radio/Stanley jumps up and, crossing to the radio, turns it off/She [Blanche] turns the knobs on the radio and it begins to play "Wien, Wien, nur du allein."/He crosses to the small white radio and snatches it off the table. With a shouted oath, he tosses the instrument out the window/ There is the sound of a blow/Something is overturned with a crash/Sounds of blows are heard.

The water goes on full tilt/The Negro entertainers in the bar around the corner play "Paper Doll" slow and blue/An indistinguishable shrill voice is heard. He hurls phone to floor. Dissonant brass and piano sounds as the rooms dim out to darkness and the outer walls appear in the night light. The "blue piano" plays for a brief interval/She [Eunice] slams her door/The low-tone clarinet moans. The door upstairs opens again/The music fades away. (Williams 2004)

- Think about the placement of the music: what does it add to the play by ways of emotional intensity, balance, and atmosphere? What does each cue signify? How integral is it to the furthering of the plot? How does it affect the nature of the characters' relationships?
- Decide if the aural environment of your production will be based entirely on Williams's suggestions or if you are also going to use additional music and sound.
- Are there any pieces that are particularly interesting to you and why? Justify your choice to combine existing music with original composition, or, reversely, to ignore Williams's directions for music.

Activity 4. Auralizing

Think of a play that is "heavy on sound," that is, one in which sound and music are either amply marked up in the stage directions or suggested in the dialogue and the action. Shakespeare's *Macbeth* (1606) could make for an attractive choice, with its sweeping mythical landscapes, the transitions between the outside and the inside, the appearance of the Three Weird Sisters and the conjuring up of magic, the creepy banging on the Porter's door and the sudden materialization of Banquo's ghost. You can start by considering the central motifs you wish to underline and work on them musically.

- What kind of atmosphere would you like to create?
- What would be the first sound elements that come to mind?

- Will you use live sound or will everything be prerecorded?
- What kind of mood or images does the play conjure up? Translating them into sounds is the backbone of the sound design process.
- What actual sound cues is the play giving you? (Think about the knocks on the Porter's gate, the screeching of birds, the horns, and drums of battle.)

Activity 5. Radio Plays

Choose one of Samuel Beckett's radio plays (*All that Fall*, *Embers*, *Words and Music*, and *Cascando*). Think of how you would approach them, considering above all the atmosphere you wish to evoke and the playwright's directions.

- What is the emotional impact you wish your sound design to generate?
- Will you keep all the sounds provided by the playwright, and if not, why?
- Will you add more sound or music and if so, why?
- Are you going to amplify the actors' voices through use of microphones?
- Would you consider using live music?
- Would you move-direct your actors or simply record them reading the text seated? How would the physical aspect influence line delivery?

Activity 6. Sound and Mood

Select a scene from your play of choice—preferably one strong on mood and subtext—and have your group research different sounds, musical periods, and styles to support the scene. Experiment with variations in rhythm, pitch, and timing of sound to achieve a different feel for different moments of the scene. A memory play (see Harold Pinter's *Old Times*) would be ideal for this exercise.

Practice 3. Sound Checklist for Directors

The following checklist can be shared between directors and sound designers during the different stages of their collaboration. It functions as a basis for settling the production's sound requirements and can be modified or developed further to serve the needs of each project. Before starting the conversation with your designer, consider the following aspects of sound design:

Use of live music, prerecorded sound, or a combination of both

Overall production style

Length of scenes for background music

Duration of sound cues or music

Exact placement of sound cues

Fade ins and fade outs of music

Quality of sound effect (harsh, smooth, etc.)

Source (where onstage or in the auditorium the sound is coming from)

Equipment (whether speakers are required)

Need for microphones

Directionality of sound (speakers concealed in the set)

Genre and period (historical, contemporary, timeless) of the play

Use of sound effects (alarm ringtones, thunder, dogs barking, etc.) and background music

Style of the music (realistic, abstract, etc.)

Location onstage from which the effects will originate

Technology

In our discussion of textuality, reference was made to how the use of technology onstage adds a complex compositional dimension to what is usually termed "visual dramaturgy." In addressing issues of identity and self-definition, digital articulation synthesizes narratives that transcend the inherent constraints of the theatre form. Engaging the aesthetic of the media, combining live and interceded presence, recorded voice, and TV-like segmentation of storytelling, technology is omnipresent in video screens, microphones, audience headphones, live cameras, remote controls, and podcasts. It encourages live performance to compete against the speed of the moving image and to accelerate, annul, or blur time and space.

The realm of technologized theatre is no longer the exclusive prerogative of an avant-garde elite of artists. A high number of contemporary directors, operating in different genres, styles, and budgets, collaborate with video designers to incorporate the media aesthetic well into live performance. Visual and auditory framing is used to not only introduce elements of the documented reality as well as different forms of art but also extend, challenge, and reconfigure the performers' subjectivity. More importantly, the use of digital media onstage creates a new relationship between performer and spectator, which is independent of the physical immediacy of the actor, and forces the audience to reconcile material presence and immaterial image. For that matter, faces and bodies can be split, multiplied, and manipulated, reinforcing the character-performer's state of liminality, an existence caught between corporeality and imagination. Increasingly, digital technology has become a firm principle—sometimes, a prerequisite—of production design, encouraging alternative forms of representing character and situation. At the same time, the Internet is exploited for its multicontextual nature, the ability to build even more widespread communities of spectators from a distance. Media-based operations are also integrated into more traditional forms of practice, occasioning jarring, and ontologically striking collisions.

Whether it features as a simple projection of still images at the back wall of a black box theatre space, prerecorded action played back on a TV screen, or more sophisticated digital forms, technology is frequently inseparable from theatrical design. And as in all other aspects of production, a meeting between director, set, costume, lighting, and video designer should be arranged early on, to get everyone on the same design plate. On a technical level, director and video designer will discuss the type and number of images (photography or videos) to be used in performance, together with the projection surface (a TV monitor, a scrim, the walls or floor of the theatre, the actor's body, etc.). One of the objectives is also to think of practical clues for high-resolution projections, without sacrificing valuable lighting or blocking choices. For technology to blend organically into the production concept, additional meetings will be scheduled over the course of rehearsals to monitor the progress of the video design.

Directing a multimedia piece has several challenges: microphones may end up sounding weak, projectors sometimes fail as their lamps die, scrims might hang wrinkled, and a Wi-Fi connection can suddenly go. However bold its use, technology is an exceptionally delicate element of staging and tends to be a relatively unreliable medium. Test it tirelessly and handle with care, to make sure it survives the crises of live performance.

At times, the media element can appear forced, imposed as an indispensable marker and accessory of artistic innovation, as opposed to a crucial facet of interpretation. The distinction between an initially audacious but ultimately cold, cerebral concept and an experiment that evolves organically into something abstract but eloquent, is fragile. So, for technology to complement and not entirely subsume the verbal and visual narrative, the motivation behind its use should also be based on the desire for discovery. The interactivity of different spaces, of the actual performance space and the digital space of imagination, is established gradually, together with the performers, the first agents of its meaningfulness and, in the end, of its viability.

A Quick Word on Adventurous Spatialities

First and foremost, what determines the director's configuration of performance space is the desired stage-auditorium relationship. Different architectural arrangements have prevailed in theatre history, with the eminent example of the Proscenium, which has the actor face the audience directly, separated by an imagined frame. In the Arena Stage, the spectators circle the playing area, surrounding the action. In the Thrust structure, the stage extends over to the spectators, who sit on three sides. The Alley typically features two rows of spectators who sit on the two sides of a long playing area, facing each other across the action that happens in-between them. Finally, the Black Box is an open, flexible space, consisting of four walls and a floor, usually painted black.

Theatre practice today has developed beyond those architectural structures, beyond even the confines of existing, inflexible buildings. Performances that travel outside conventional theatres have rendered scenography a constitutive element of storytelling. In site-specific theatre, the action is transferred to spaces that typically serve different functions (such as parking lots, churches, warehouses, public swimming pools, bars and hotel rooms, among the few). Notably, the communication between the audience and the stage is reconsidered, given the absence of the latter component of the pair. The dialogue is now between spectator and event, and the levels of engagement that exist in their encounter, particularly because working in non-theatre spaces has "challenged theatre designers to confront and rethink communicative assumptions" (McKinney and Butterworth 2009, 120). Unconventional performing spaces create opportunities for visionary experiences, and new spatial adventures urge spectators to participate more fully into actions of which they are not only witnesses but also active makers.

As theatre turns to novel forms of representing reality and, ultimately, of spectating, so is scenography redefined as a concept and practice. Unstable, shifting, ever-transforming *sites* replace the frontal, bidirectional comforts of the proscenium arch. These sites "possess their own aesthetic qualities and their own histories and even though they may be adapted to accommodate specific performances, inherent characteristics remain" (McKinney and Butterworth 2009, 122). Rather than rely of structures of design that will support the imaginary world of the play, many directors and designers set out to reframe the "real," existing space, so that it can release its age-proof energies and interact intimately with the text, its new guest. This practice goes hand-in-hand with the conviction that whatever the genre or style, any text can be physicalized and fully amalgamated into the outside world. No longer a fiction, it is transformed into a real-time, real-space occurrence of life, a story that is both poeticized and rendered familiar by merely being placed away from the archetypical locus of illusion, the authoritative theatre stage and its auditorium.

The spatially innovative work of artists such as Welsh theatre maker Mike Pearson or companies such as the British Punchdrunk and New York-based Third Rail Projects, among many others, continues to push the boundaries of traditional theatre-going experience. The same holds for Fruit for the Apocalypse—a company that operates between London and Rotterdam—whose productions are self-characterized as "audiokinetic adventures in Opera, Ballet and Composition" (http://www.fruit-for-the-apocalypse.eu/#stories). The group is best known for their 24/7 performance project, The Surrealist Taxi, in which spectators get picked up by a taxi and must determine the direction and length of their drive by drawing from a deck of cards. Being a spectator-participant in those performances can be an extraordinary, exhilarating, if often uncomfortable, experience. Take, for example, Punchdrunk's New York production of *Sleep No More* (2011), an imaginative take on Shakespeare's *Macbeth*. The masked spectators wander up and down the stairs, corridors, and furniture-cluttered rooms of the dimly lit, 1930s McKittrick Hotel in Manhattan and watch the bloodstained action of the play unfold in no specific order.

Just as directing matures further into an art of interminable exploration and discovery and embraces even more unorthodox forms of staging, so does the spectator become more adventurous and uninhibited. The audience begins to share more with the performer, celebrating an atmosphere of mutual occasion and community. The term *immersive*, which applies to various participatory theatre events, is a direct reference to the engagement of the senses in a visceral and typically interactive involvement with performance. Spectators are

> expected to be alert, engaged, involved and prepared for invigoration...put their psychological and physiological capabilities to work, either through some form of physical exertion, or through an intimate involvement in performance that enlivens the affective possibilities of an uncertain future.
>
> (Alston 2016, 3)

In such nonmainstream forms—in which theatre evolves from a free narrative or theme, as opposed to a preexisting script as such—the production design develops in tandem with the story or the text. Scenography has now become a catalytic presence in the synthetic, synchronic, and organic orchestration of the theatre event.

WORKBOOK 5.3

Practice I. Exploring Found Space

Working with found space can be extremely fun and creative. The following exercise is an invitation to imagine buildings or locations that could conceivably host spatially enterprising readings of plays. Research by means of field trips and an exploration of different sites is just as necessary as is resourcefulness—the ability to transform given/found spaces beyond their established and predictable uses.

Activity I. Site-Specific Metaphors

Make a list of plays that could yield an interesting site-specific staging. Think outside obvious examples (such as Edward Albee's *The Zoo Story*, set on a park bench, or Agatha Christie's interactive play *The Mousetrap*, set in an atmospheric Victorian Manor House in the English countryside).

Review the spatial metaphors you will employ
and imagine the kind of spaces/public sites/
buildings/locations that could accommodate your
interpretation.

What is the rationale behind each choice?

How actively involved do you wish your audience to be?

How would you rate the level of difficulty in staging your
site-specific show?

Activity 2. Site-Specific Readings

Create a *site-specific* version of your play of choice to express:

- A political reading
- An interactive rapport with the audience
- A parody

Activity 3. Immersive Experiences

Think of a story that would make for a strong immersive
theatre experience.

Consider the potential setting and the characters
involved.

Write the first scene of a new play, taking into account specific roles or functions that you will be assigning to the spectators.

Try staging this scene in front of an audience of friends and colleagues, and make sure you include some of the insights gained into a fuller script.

WORKS CITED

Alston, Adam. *Beyond Immersive Theatre*. New York: Palgrave Macmillan, 2016.

Aronson, Arnold. *Looking into the Abyss*. Ann Arbor: The University of Michigan Press, 2008.

Complicite. Web. 5 July 2017. http://www.complicite.org/productions/theen counter.

Erven, Charles. "Hand in Glove: The Designer as Director as Designer," in *Directors and Designers*. Ed. White, Christine A. Bristol: Intellect, 2009.

Fruit for the Apocalypse. Web. 19 September 2017. http://www.fruit-for-the-apocalypse.eu/#stories.

Hodge, Francis. 1971. *Play Directing. Analysis, Communication, and Style*. Fourth Edition. Englewood Cliffs, NJ: Prentice Hall, 1994.

Howard, Pamela. *What Is Scenography?* London and New York: Routledge, 2001.

Howard, Pamela. "Directors and Designers. Is There a Different Direction?" in *The Potentials of Spaces. The Theory and Practice of Scenography & Performance*. Eds. Oddey, Alison and Christine White. Bristol: Intellect, 2006.

Jones, Robert Edmund. 1941. *The Dramatic Imagination. Reflections and Speculations on the Art of the Theatre*. New York and London: Routledge, 2004.

Kay, Deena and James LeBrecht. *Sound and Music for the Theatre*. Third Edition. Oxford: Focal Press, 2009.

Marranca, Bonnie, ed. *The Theatre of Images*. New York: Drama Book Specialists, 1977.

McKinney, Joslin and Philip Butterworth. *The Cambridge Introduction to Scenography*. Cambridge: Cambridge University Press, 2009.

Oddey, Alison and Christine White. *The Potentials of Spaces. The Theory and Practice of Scenography & Performance*. Bristol: Intellect, 2006.

Pavis, Patrice. *Languages of the Stage*. New York: Performing Arts Journal Publications, 1993.

Ubersfeld, Anne. *Reading Theatre*. Toronto and London: University of Toronto Press, 1999.

White, Christine A., ed. *Directors and Designers*. Bristol: Intellect, 2009.

Williams, Tennessee. *A Streetcar Named Desire*. New York: A New Directions Book, 2004.

Chapter 6

Director and Actor

Acting as Directing

It has been variously stated that meaningful acting is not an imitation of behavior, but a conscious immersion into a fiction that must be made to appear truthful. In British sculptor Henry Moore's elegant formulation, the creation of art is likened to "maybe a penetration into reality" as opposed to an escape from life (in Herbert 2000, 174). Actors imagine, recall, risk, adapt, justify, and communicate, leaving a part of themselves behind, to transform into somebody else, an authentic "other." They use imagination to *visualize* and their trained expressive means (body and voice) to *physicalize* character. In this process, they are not alone. Directors and actors are together in forming entire worlds and human presences onstage. Over the course of this, their relationship matures from one of parent-child to that of two equal partners wishing to maintain a healthy and exciting connection in the span of their shared lifetime. More than anything, this relationship is based on a condition of mutual license because, as Ostermeier reveals, the prime function of the director is to describe and communicate with the actor.

> You discuss a dialogue, you agree on a situation in a play – and then it's up to the actor. [...] When something happens in rehearsals which I don't control, when something is liberated in the actors, then I leave the rehearsal room in bliss. I don't get that from feeling 'fine, my concept works.'
>
> (In Delgado and Rebellato 2010, 355)

Ideally, directors guide and support the actor in making discoveries and becoming a better director of character.

Actors and Actors

Training, Methods, Technique

Some (very brief) history of acting is due here, to provide context to our discussion of actor preparation. As early as the beginning of the twentieth century, a strong interest in the actor emerged forcefully, in tandem with innovative forms of stagecraft and theories about the revised role of both director and performer. Major approaches to acting—as were notably those propounded by Stanislavski, Meyerhold, Copeau, Brecht, the followers of the American Method, Grotowski and Brook, among others—sprang up from different corners of the world. Practice-based theories eventually became training systems, which were to influence the art of acting in the years to come, and propagate additional, hybrid forms of practice. Those systems were based on different philosophies of acting, the presence of theatre in society and the function of the director-actor binary within performance.

Irrespective of their distinct outlook on the art of acting, most theatre theorists and practitioners seemed to share a common pursuit, that is, to prepare actors to achieve truthfulness onstage, whether by looking inward or by exploiting the inexhaustible potential of the body. For Stanislavski, the first actor-director to systematically theorize acting, psychological resources were to be explored together with physical actions. Meyerhold, on the other hand, reacting against naturalistic representation, codified physical movement and produced several biomechanical exercises meant to release meaning through physical agility and competence. In a different context, Brecht's Epic Theatre viewed actors as agents of a political message, who served the mission to awaken audiences to pressing social issues, without, however questioning the sincerity of acting. In the 1960s and 1970s, Jerzy Grotowski's emphasis on a performance style based on ritualistic and spiritual simplicity led to the lifelong ambition of freeing actors from psychophysical constraints in order to expand their expressive range.

These and other systems have been passed down, either in their original form or in variations, as important parts of actors' formal education and directors' rehearsal strategies. Choosing the right training for one's physical and mental disposition is an actor's job, although professionals are quite competent at most aspects of the leading acting methods, which duly renders them fully operational in different rehearsal contexts. Similarly, despite the fact that experienced practitioners tend to favor one acting mode over another, they will usually borrow different training principles to serve specific production demands and the general makeup and background of the cast. In this sense, the richness and value of any approach seem to lie in their ability to operate autonomously but also in conjunction with other methodologies.

With all the diverse stylistic influences at work in any given project, you can eventually develop your own method and keep revising it, trying out new techniques or incorporating existing elements from other established practices.

Training is necessary for setting up and perfecting technique, which is where talent and imagination grow. It supports actors in using their body and voice expressively, without unnecessary restraint, and in a personally satisfying manner. Conquering any technique designed to develop the actor's body, voice, and emotional and intellectual aptitude happens slowly over time. It involves learning and practicing different skills—the most basic being breathing, handling speech, rhythm, timing, singing, dancing, and stage combat—but also developing confidence and stage presence. Relying on impulse alone can make an actor unpredictable and, so, the safety of technique is particularly critical in those unfortunate moments when a real emotive connection to character seems to falter.

Technique is the full exploitation of the physical and vocal resources so that imagination can take over. It helps actors master control of their body and their voice, which starts with knowing when to breathe and, through training and practice, affects all aspects of their presence onstage. In the end, technique makes talent visible and lasting.

Preparation: Building Self and Character

Actors and characters meet on a leap of faith. For some, character is simply one person's text uttered in the context of a dramatic situation. Mamet's aphorism is once again telling: "The actor does not need to 'become' the character. The phrase, in fact, has no meaning. There *is* no character. They are lines of dialogue meant to be said by the actor" (1999, 9–10). To most actors, nonetheless, "character" is a new skin into which they will have to change at regular intervals. Acclaimed American actor Willem Dafoe explains that even when has a character, he is always curious to see how he reads, what people think he is, and who he is, and then he lays the action on top of that so he is confronting himself in these circumstances:

It's open-ended. I'm not presenting anything; I'm feeling my way through. If you were acting something, if you were very conscious of acting a character, somewhere you would close it down, you'd present it. You'd finish it. In this stuff, you never know.

(Qtd in Zarrilli 2002, 307)

For audiences, each character onstage is another projection of our relationship with the world. No matter how one defines it, a role is always infused with the performer's personality, which makes interpretation for both actor and spectator a fluctuating operation, ever unstable and prone to disruption and transformation. No matter how intensely characters and actors merge, the ghost of the self will always pursue the actor, bearing with it an element of chance and precariousness. Transcending the theatrical illusion, the audience will also see the actor behind the character, and in many legendary performances, character and actor will be identified as one entity. It is nearly impossible, for example, to think about the character of Stanley Kowalski without conjuring up Marlon Brando's mercurial presence in his white T-shirt and jeans in Elia Kazan's Broadway production (1947) and film (1951) of *A Streetcar Named Desire*.

Moreover, for an actor, talent is inseparable from imagination, which describes the ability to conceive of character and situation instinctually, and absorb a fictitious reality macroscopically as well as microscopically. Granted, directors have little control over the actors' innate resourcefulness, but they can still try to alert them to different possibilities of interpretation, however counterintuitive these may seem. Can the actor playing Chekhov's Vanya also appear "cool" and energetic? What would these qualities add to the part? Would you have the actress performing Blanche reveal a crass face underneath the damsel persona? As a director, you may be cautious of the very term "character," but you still need to navigate the actor through the more intricate stations of the script, advise them on the movement of the dialogue and the energy of each line, and present options that undermine familiar or cliché representation.

In rehearsal, you help actors reveal their character to the public. The two have probably already become acquainted during their more private encounters, where the actor seduces the character into materializing; now, you can examine together how the role connects to the environment, the moment in time and the other characters, and simply respond to the play, its geography and climate, the season, time of the day, and changing locations. Together, also, you will do research, both as keen observers of human behavior, and by taking full advantage of libraries, museums and art galleries, the Internet, or the cinema. This is good bonding time, which happily bridges the original setting of the play with the present. And, of course, no character can ever develop in a void. It may be hard to get an actor performing Goethe's Faust to suddenly have a natural-sounding conversation with the Devil, not least in verse. Have him or her improvise with different possible contexts (falling asleep in a research lab, getting drunk in a shabby bar, sweating in a game of squash, etc.), and bounce off the actor playing conflicting and surprising aspects of Mephistopheles (sinister and cynical but also playful and affectionate). On all accounts, be there and open a different door for your actors to step through.

Beware of Emotions (At Least Onstage!)

Sooner or later, the character will move into the actor's body and occupy that space for as long as the rehearsals and the performances last. For an actor, this is a powerful moment, a breakthrough that you should cherish. Without a doubt, actors need you to acknowledge the effort and the talent that has gone into this transformation, so that they can then experience their part without anxiety or guilt, avoiding imitations of behavior or "playing emotion" compulsively. In fact, there is perhaps nothing more distressing than watching an actor struggle to force emotion and nothing more powerful than being moved before the actor even looks visibly affected. Think about Blanche and her breakdown "Death is expensive, Miss Stella" monologue in Scene 1 of *A Streetcar*, in which she describes to her sister her miserable life in *Belle Reve*, where she had to bury her sick relatives, one after another. Think further of her heart-wrenching "Allan monologue" in Scene 6, where she confesses her young husband's suicide to her suitor Mitch. How can an actor pull those through without collapsing into sentimentalism?

It's good to be reminded that in real life, discoveries can happen to us while we are busy doing ordinary things and that the actors' job is to focus on the moment and follow the dramatic energy through, letting the emotional life take care of itself. Instead of watching them fake their tears in different degrees of successful imitation, you can suggest physical actions, which can directly connect them with the text, the character, the other actors, and the other characters. Give the actress playing Blanche something physical to hang onto: in Scene 1, this could be the obvious drinking routine, unpacking her suitcase, applying make-up, etc., or simply refilling her glass and opening the window in Scene 6. You can also have her fight an uncomfortable state, such as drunkenness, pure exhaustion, or the urge to burst into tears. As spectators, we enjoy partaking of the actors' real-time, moment-to-moment growth, which is a way of witnessing how they gradually change out of the self and into the character. In fact, it is immensely satisfying to follow an idea, an argument, or a resolution unfold as a result of the actor's thought process and the intelligent handling of speech.

The more specific and detailed the actions are, the richer will be the acting. An actor who is focused on what he or she does, unconcerned with showing emotion but concentrated on what goes on in the present moment of the moment is bound to give the scene its due intensity.

WORKBOOK 6.1

Practice 1. Art Fun

The following activities are meant to induce childlike, uncensored fun. They can be used in the early stages of rehearsals when the company is still experimenting with characterization and play analysis. They can be applied as a warm-up at the beginning of rehearsal or during a break, after an intense session of table work.

Activity 1. Drawing the Character

Bring paper, pencils, and crayons to rehearsal, and gather your actors in the room. Give them plenty of time to come up with an image of their character. It can be anything as small as a doodle or a more sophisticated drawing that presents the character in full costume and detail.

Have the actors pass around their visuals and ask the rest of the group to comment on what they perceive the personality of each character to be from the clues they get from the drawing.

Activity 2. Storyboarding

Bring paper, pencils, and crayons to rehearsal. Gather all your actors together around a table and ask them to go through each scene of the play and make a sketch or a drawing of the main dramatic event. If the script is long and has many scenes, they can storyboard the principal ones.

Allow plenty of time (a minimum of 30'), and when everyone's more or less finished, have the group share each other's work and discuss the main points of focus for each actor, according to their drawing.

Practice 2. Character Work

The following rehearsal techniques—often used in variations and under different names—suggest ways of understanding character and are useful for the actor's preparation, either as homework (Activities 1 and 2) or as part of group table work (Activities 3 and 4).

Activity I. Know the Objectives

Working on a scene from your play of choice, ask your actors to go through carefully scene and unit objectives. Are they are part of the broader super objective? Have them share their thoughts with the group. Pay attention to possible contradictions, confusing or ambivalent choices, or any patterns emerging.

The following is an example from the Prologue and the first episode of *Oedipus Rex* (verses 1–462). Here, Oedipus addresses the dismayed people of Thebes and investigates King Laius' murder.

- Oedipus' Super Objective: to discover the murder of Laius.
- Oedipus' Unit Objective 1: to convince the Chorus elders to help him find the murderer of Laius.
- Oedipus Unit Objective 2: to get the blind soothsayer Tiresias to reveal the secret about Laius' murderer.

Activity 2. Know the Obstacles

In your play of choice, have your actors create a detailed list of the obstacles (internal and external) that keep the characters from getting what they want. Ask them to analyze the characters' strategies to overcome the challenges and achieve their objectives. Here is a brief analysis of *Uncle Vanya's* obstacles in Chekhov's title play:

Example: "In *Uncle Vanya*, the key characters seem distressed about their lives and find it difficult to react against the sense of stagnation and lost dreams. Vanya wants to change his life but he lacks the inner drive to do it. His obstacles are both external (he is obliged to continue taking care of the estate and to manage its finances) and internal: he appears mentally, morally, and psychologically exhausted. Essentially, he is too passive and embittered to handle his grievances effectively."

Activity 3. Gather Information

In your play of choice, have your actors list all the information that the playwright provides about their character. They should compose one list of the external and internal character traits, and another list of all the physical actions that are described in the stage directions and in the dialogue. The following is an example from the opening stage directions of *Death of a Salesman*. The list is for Willy Loman:

What he does:

- He enters, carrying two large sample cases.
- He crosses to the doorway of the house.
- He unlocks the door.
- He comes into the kitchen and lets his burden down.
- He feels the soreness of his palms.
- He sighs "Oh boy, oh, boy."
- He closes the door. He carries his cases out into the living room through the kitchen doorway.

The way he looks:

- He is past 60 years of age, dressed quietly.
- His exhaustion is apparent.

In the dialogue

- [Casual irritation]
- Willy: "I'm tired to death."
- Linda to Willy: "You look terrible."
- Willy: "I'm, I can't seem to – keep my mind to it."

Activity 4. What Is My Story?

After the first *read-through* of your play of choice, ask your actors to write down their character's story in one paragraph. Invite them to read their piece out loud. They should be advised to keep this bit of writing together with their actors' notes.

After the play's first *run-through*, have the actors write their character's story once again and then go back to their first piece of writing. Has anything changed? How has the actor's impression of the character developed, if at all?

Activity 5. In Someone Else's Shoes

To help actors get a better sense of the other characters and the relationships that have evolved among them, you could have them read through a crucial scene of your play of choice, changing roles. For instance, the actor playing Willy in *Death of a Salesman can* read Biff's lines, Happy can read for Willy, and so on. In scenes where a bigger cast is involved you may have all the women read the male parts and vice versa.

- When the actors finish reading, ask the group to reflect on what they gained from this brief encounter with the other character/s.
- Then, have them go back to the scene and reread it, this time in their "own" character. Was their perspective on the scene at all influenced by the experience of being in someone else's shoes?

Activity 6. Updating

Encourage your actors to consider their character within the play's historical circumstances. In the case of a period play, have them reimagine their character in the present time and make a drawing that depicts them dressed up in today's clothes and carrying contemporary accessories and props (laptops, smartphones, etc.). The more detailed these sketches are, the better.

Directing Actors

In Rehearsal: Directors, Actors, Text

The rehearsal space is akin to a construction site for you and your actors. A period of table work and blocking, the length of which depends on the complexity of the project, the script, and the working style of each director, eventually leads to a series of run-throughs where all the work is bound to come together in a more or less unified whole. This is the time to resolve major logistical headaches, but also action and character-related issues, before the show moves to tech week. Acting coach and director Brigid Panet compares rehearsing to

> the making of a jigsaw: after the first look at the picture on the box (the whole play), we break it up into small pieces, each of which has its own place and must be joined to all the pieces around it. As rehearsals progress to the performance, each of these separate pieces must be joined together seamlessly to form the correct picture.
>
> (Panet 2009, 94)

Other than discussing character, theme, and point of view, table work, as we saw, concerns the close analysis of the play. For many rehearsals, you can follow Stanislavski either devotedly or more freely and break down the entire text into units and beats, so that the given circumstances, character objectives, and actions form a common foundation of understanding the world of the play. While the actor has plenty of homework to do after leaving the room, you should be concerned with getting everybody connected to the text. However, given that the same questions will be addressed again and again during the blocking phase, you needn't spend too much time on extensive conversation. Instead, get people on their feet soon. Most of the times, simply observing how the scene develops physically will help you pin it much more organically than by furiously jotting down notes on your script alone, cut off from the kind of collaborative work that encourages discoveries.

Five Wh-s and One H-, or Handling the "Givens"

Just as directors interpret the text from within a specific concept or form, actors develop their characters when they are fully acclimatized to the conditions that surround them. Soon after reading the play for the first time and vigorously highlighting their lines in their scripts, they begin to form their personal set of circumstances more or less automatically, alongside those already provided by the playwright. In fact, character list making—recommended by the director or as part of their private work at home—is a popular actor task. Shortly after the initial phases of table work, the *why* and *how* of each action can now complement the analysis of the basic "Wh-questions" (*who, what, where, when*). This comprehensive set, further to summarizing the fundamentals aspects of story and setting, also leads actors to inferences that can help them approach their role less predictably. In times of doubt, you can always point their attention back to this list as a means of grounding the character on the world of the play.

What	• *What is the play about? What happens in it? What is the story of each character? What does the character want? What does the character do to get what he or she wants?*
Where	• *Where is the action of the play taking place (geographical location)? Where is every scene happening (indoors vs. outdoors, home vs. work, countryside, seaside, urban environment, unknown locale, other)?*
When	• *When is the action of the play taking place (period/year, season, time of the day, and the historical and political context)? When is every scene happening (time elapsing between acts and scenes)?*
Who	• *Who is in the play (dramatis personae, relationships among them)? Who is your character (information about social, educational, and economic background, family and professional status, etc.)?*
Why	• *Why was the play written? (Possible reasons—personal, ideological, aesthetic, or other—why the playwright wrote the text.) Why is the plot structured the way it is? Why do the characters act the way they do?*

	• *How did the playwright organize all the elements of the play to create a new, self-ruling universe? How are the characters constructed? How do the characters act and interact with one another?*
How	

Unit-ing and Action-ing

The significance of character objectives and actions in any discussion of dramaturgy has already been pointed out. To the actor, in particular, these terms are major challenges to address over the course of rehearsing, and therefore, even if you, the director, are to have the final say in how a scene should be broken down, it is wise to involve your actors in the *unit-ing* process. Actions, which are meant to affect the opposing character to feel something specific, must be matched with objectives and differ from one unit to another. In rehearsal, as characterization develops, they are usually applied physically and are discarded or replaced if proven ineffective or unsuitable in the context of the scene. And, as has been also stressed, it is subtext—what a character does not say but experiences in any given moment of the dialogue—that will activate a specific action, beyond what is stated verbally. If anything, the inner life of the character is a lot more than the sum of the spoken words. Here is another example from *Death of a Salesman*, which brings the conflict between Willy and Biff to a point of explosion through subtext, alone:

> [Text] WILLY (TO BIFF): If you get tired hanging around tomorrow, paint the ceiling I put up in the living room.
> [*Subtext*] *You're so lazy, all you do is sit around doing nothing.*
> [Text] BIFF: I'm leaving early tomorrow.
> [*Subtext*]: *I'm finally getting away from all this.*
>
> (1986, 49)
>
> [Text] WILLY: The door of your life is wide open!
> [*Subtext*] *Please give me something to hold onto!*
>
> (1986, 105)

The most intuitive actors will know that in order to commit to an action they must connect energetically to the objective that precedes it. As a result, they try to justify rather than criticize the character they are embodying. Your responsibility here is to ask questions that reveal aspects of the character of which the actor seems to be ignorant or to which he or she seems indifferent. Furthermore, it is to "kill" any assumptions about character as soon as they are born. The dreaded motto "my character would never do that," which most directors have at some point or other been warned against, is simply another way of saying "I [the actor] refuse to do that."

> The inner justification of an action is a golden rule for both directors and actors. Every gesture, movement, and physical attitude is a statement about how the character reacts to a new situation. It is meaning communicated visually. In fact, everything that the director suggests and the actor enacts onstage is a sign and a seed of interpretation and, ideally, the result of keen reflection.

One way of looking at actions is as a means to get one character to feel or react against an original "provocation" by another character. Such an exchange of reactions, intended to move the plot forward, is framed through active verbs, including the likes of "persuade," "seduce," "apologize," "humiliate," "threaten," "forgive," "confess," and so forth. *Action-ing* is the operation of going through the script and finding an active, transitive verb for each line of the text. The following are some examples illustrating the connection between character objectives and actions. They are drawn from the usual suspects of the Western dramatic canon, to some of which we have already referred. Note the correspondence between objectives in different moments of the play and the actions these generate:

- *Objective*: Oedipus wants to get Tiresias to reveal the truth about the murder of Laius.
  Action: Oedipus interrogates Tiresias/threatens Tiresias.
- *Objective*: Medea wants to punish Jason for betraying her.
  Action: Medea hurts Jason/kills her children.
- *Objective*: Linda wants to comfort Willy.
  Action: Linda convinces Willy to forgive Biff.
- *Objective: Miss Julie* wants to break free of her confinement.
  Action: Miss Julie seduces Jean.
- *Objective:* Nora wants to start a new life.
  Action: Nora prepares Torvald to accept her decision to leave.

Actors will usually try actions out in physical terms, experimenting with movement and gesture, but also with voice, intonation, and pitch. This leads to a stage when you will be focusing on more detailed work, ordinarily referred to as *business*, the small, practical activities that underline the action of a unit or scene. They may include standard domestic routines such as mopping, reading a book, typing, getting dressed or setting the table, playing an instrument or singing, or other undertakings involving sophisticated choreography (special dances, fighting, etc.) or expert skills (painting, playing sports, handling machinery). Once again, you should be there to observe the actor's work and suggest alternatives where you feel the action lacks in clarity or impact. It goes without saying that all through the play and the individual scenes, actions will keep changing, as obstacles get in the way. Addressing a new obstacle shifts the action from one unit to the next, giving the character the incentive to push through impediments and evolve dynamically. After all, the character, as Ostermeier tells us, "only ever makes an attempt to adapt to the situation and respond to the problem he or she is confronted with" (qtd in Boenisch and Ostermeier 2016, 189).

Emotion Memory

To some extent, most directors will apply (some do so systematically, others, ad hoc) parts of Stanislavski's stipulations concerning script analysis, concentration or working with physical actions. One essential but also controversial principle of the system is to have the actor recall memories and then apply them to the role, a technique that psychologically trained actors find instrumental to character building. And while unit-ing and action-ing are carried out jointly with the director, *emotion memory*—also known as *affective memory*—is an actor's personal way of relating to the role instinctually. The main premise is that actors look back to events from their past that may contain emotions similar to the ones their character is currently experiencing and which they may apply to different moments of the play as a way of accessing their role more directly. For all its powerful influence on actor preparation, emotion memory is not meant to replace the character's present moment with the actor's private life. Simply put, it is a stimulus for character development and not a sacrifice of character to self. If you work with method actors, you must be cautious of its (over)use and intervene to stop an actor from indulging, in case the memory becomes overwhelming.

In Rehearsal: Directors, Actors, Stage

Learning Lines

By the time the table work period is more or less over, the company will move to the blocking phase, where characters and actions will be created physically. As a rule, some directors will have requested of their actors to know their lines already by the first rehearsal, while others may be more sympathetic to the need for a more gradual, organic course, where the text is learned alongside the movement. There are different advantages and disadvantages in each approach, but consistency is a must. At least as far as learning lines goes, be clear on when exactly you expect the actor to be off-book.

Warm-ups

Before actors get on their feet, you may give them some time to relax their muscles and prepare their bodies for physical scene work. Often, there is a 10- or 15-minute workout at the beginning of rehearsal for each actor individually or with the whole group getting together for additional bonding time. Sometimes, especially when the company members are still new to each other, you can offer to lead the warm-up session yourself, and introduce new exercises targeted to specific rehearsal goals. One idea is to have the actors work alternately with relaxation and voice exercises or yoga and more rigorous movement techniques (e.g., biomechanical exercises or the *Viewpoints*). Such combinations of seemingly incompatible practices can release vocal and body tensions, build concentration and also foster a group ethic. A good warm-up should ideally leave the actor relaxed but energetic and eager to interact with the ensemble.

Improvisations

While the scene is being blocked and characters formulated, directors regularly initiate improvisational exercises, as a shortcut to the imagined reality of the play. Improvisation usually concerns performing a scene using your own words as opposed to the existing text, which also generates fresh actions. It is instrumental for examining character status (one character's power and influence over another), keeping the stakes of the play up, solving practical problems or complex relationship dynamics and improving the ensemble spirit. In general, there are different types of improvisation, each serving a different function. It should be noted, however, that not every actor responds well to its spontaneous, get-up-and-go imperative. Typically, younger actors are more open to trying things out, even at the risk of looking or sounding ridiculous. Older actors tend to rely more on technique and are often reluctant to venture into spot-on group games. As usual, you need to strike the right balance without alienating any of the actors. Suggest improvisations if you suspect there is trouble with a text's heavily poetic language or if an actor is struggling with a particularly convoluted monologue. When the target is clear, doing the scene in "your own words," can connect actors to their characters, encouraging them to be spontaneous, daring, and even "wrong." Control and interrupt improvisations the moment they degenerate to aimless explorations or make the actor idle and no longer connected to the text.

Movement and Gesture

Many theatre artists across the twentieth and twenty-first centuries have developed their own systems of actor movement. Obviously, it would be pointless to summarize in a few lines how Laban Movement Analysis (LMA) systematizes human movement or describe how Jacques LeCoq's mime and mask training or Anne Bogart's compositional philosophy of *Viewpoints* work. Essentially, different systems of movement training examine how the body responds to the modalities of space and time.

Unlike composition and picturization, in principle defined by the director, physicalizing character is a joined director-actor affair. Movement supports character and creates the action and atmosphere of the scene, interpreting, rather than illustrating the reality in which it occurs. In the same vein, gesture, the aspect of movement that contains the physical life of one single character and actor, becomes expressive and meaningful not by how small or big it is, but by how well it manages to steer clear of trite usage. In addition, entrances and exits are part of a long history of events in the life of the character, and for movement to be resonant, you and your actors should also think about what comes before and what after a scene. According to where the character arrives from—it can be any situation as mundane as doing the dishes, as exhilarating as an early morning walk in the forest or as devastating as a late night break-up with a lover—the energy of the previous situation will inevitably sneak into the present moment. Encourage your actors to remain physically open to any emotional changes the new scene will bring.

Whatever the form, style, or rhythm of the movement, it should feel natural to the actor and true to the character and the environment, and yet remain surprising. Banal physical actions can become refreshingly unfamiliar if the dialogue contradicts them in emotional tone. A striking movement, too, protects both character and performer from the dangers of a "stagey" look. Remember, for example, Blanche's arrival to the Elysian Fields and her struggle to stand straight and remain composed in the sweltering heat of Stella's and Stanley's room. How desperate and exhausted is she, after all her traveling and the shock she experiences when first stepping into the Kowalskis' squalid premises? Consider having her wipe the sweat off her neck using the dirty dishcloth she finds lying around, while still trying to keep appearances with Eunice. After all, in real life, we engage in the most mundane activities while experiencing profound turmoil or discussing the most complex subjects. It goes without saying that, although surprise is an important goal, the movement should also feature an inner logic. Think, for example, the use of anachronistic (contemporary) gesture and movement in a period piece. Some directors are quite adept at creating moments where even the most acute contrast between what the actors say and what they do seems to make sense on an intuitive level.

With all that said, the occasional stillness onstage can relate emotional or mental movement powerfully. Action, as Stanislavski taught us, can be as minimal as an actor simply sitting onstage facing the audience. What makes some still moments especially compelling is the stamina and concentration they require of the actors to discover and justify their characters' reason for being present in the scene without moving. Again, your job as director is to determine the emotional score that drives the actor's stillness.

> Theatrical movement is influenced by various factors, including character action, status levels, the degree of dramatic intensity or release, the rhythm of delivery, and spatial considerations. It is also determined by mood—a contemplative atmosphere will usually slow down the actors' movements; costume—elaborate period costumes make particular demands on the actor; and props and set—an ambitious design involving delicate materials or precarious architectural pieces inevitably invites equally adventurous forms of blocking.

Rhythm

Is being accurate, versatile, and timely with rhythm an acquired skill? Being an agent of the play's overall energy, rhythm is the means by which a performance expresses verbally and physically the pulse of the text across dramatic time. It advances the story, structures the narrative, and gives variation and feeling to the acting and the *mise-en-scène*. Many directors are born with a good ear for rhythm and timing, and this also goes for actors. Some texts, too, are written more musically than others. In principle, handling the rhythm of the dialogue is the actor's job. Skilled professionals are trained to understand where each breath occurs. In fact, they learn their lines by processing breathing patterns that carry the meaning of the line with the right rhythmical muscle. They also know that rhythm changes when units change, being the "accumulative effect of the unit beats and is, perhaps, another way of describing surges" (Hodge 1994, 57). Tempo, on the other hand, has more to do with speed—how fast or slow we move from one beat to the next—while timing concerns the exact duration and positioning of a single action within a series of actions. In this context, pauses and repetition are additional built-in mechanisms of rhythm.

If you read a play a few times, you will be able to identify its rhythmical shape and the function and placement of speeches. Afterward, you can let the actor deal with the particulars of delivery. As far as understanding rhythm goes, Norwegian playwright Jon Fosse's *Someone is Going to Come* (1996) would be an excellent case in point. The play tells the story of a couple arriving at a remote seaside location, full of expectation to move into a new house and get away from the pressures of living in society. Soon, a fleeting impression that "someone is going to come" (2002, 16) becomes a disturbing obsession, growing into an open threat, when a man who claims to be the previous owner of the house and a neighbor, actively intrudes into the two characters' (He and She) life. Fosse compounds a poetry of violence that seems to fore-shadow and precipitate the unraveling of the plot, further to capturing the couple's torment. Featuring a unique stanza and line division, it commands an almost breathless delivery of statements and questions, which seem impossible to process at normal speed. In the following characteristic speech, a sense of urgency may be achieved by having the actor confront unapologetically its phrasal repetitions, the momentary silences, the sharp turns:

SHE
I just know
that someone is going to come
You also want for someone
to come
You would rather be together
with others than with me
You would rather be together with others
Someone is going to come
If we go in then someone will come
and knock on the door
knock and knock on the door
Someone is going to knock on the door
going to knock and knock on the door
and not give up
Just knock.

(2002, 21)

The accelerated delivery of the text, as She's dread builds up, will inevi-tably convey her disquiet. In the entire play, Fosse's staccato score of al-ternating pronouns, monosyllables, and repetitions needs to be stressed boldly in order to travel the spectator from a nebulous sensation of un-ease to a consummate experience of terror.

Because rhythm shelters emotional intensity and indicates changes in action, it is crucial to be precise about the timing and pacing of each unit. For their interactions to be well paced and the shifts in action well timed, actors should first and foremost be focused on what they do *on the beat* and stay in synch with each other. That way, they will also be ready for what the next unit brings, without appearing "prepared" or "rehearsed" for fresh observations or discoveries.

Run-throughs

Depending on the needs of the scene and the challenges of rehearsals, you may also find it useful to commit some run-throughs to a specific task. You might, for example, ask the actors to rerun a scene to clear up the blocking; revise their objectives or actions; adjust their vocal levels; or sharpen moments of dramatic tension. During a run-through, you should watch for any moments in the scene when it appears that the actors' technique overshadows their imagination. If that is indeed the case, you can try motivating the actor to implement the least predictable reading and consider the less standard response. Examples include: playing against a line; playing against the expected and "acceptable" characterization (e.g., Willy Loman's or Blanche's vulnerable moments can be invested with emphatic bouts of stubbornness and arrogance); playing against rhythm (actors can be less predictable about where to stress a line or where to pause). The fact that surprise is ultimately what keeps theatre alive and necessary can never be stressed enough.

> Acting should always reflect the chaotic textures of life, where people laugh at the most uncomfortable moments and mean things that are the exact opposite of what they say. No matter how unexpected the design or the staging, unless the actor braves habit, the performance will still move into the realm of the commonplace.

There is a point in the process where a rehearsal will start to look like a preview, usually when, upon invitation, friends and acquaintances show up to a mature run-through. In these initial encounters of stage and auditorium, you can gauge the pulse of the house in the spectators' level of engagement, their silences, quality of attention, notable gasps or breathing, and final applause. It is a terrifying moment but also an essential test of the production's energy—of your and the actor's work.

WORKBOOK 6.2

Practice 1. Character Facts

The following exercises concern the actor's work on character. They are simple ways to collect character-related information from the text, but also advocate some associative thinking, which can make characterization less predictable.

Activity 1. Character Bio (Script Version)

Have your actors compose a short biography of their character, based on the information in the script. Where applicable, ask them to make a list of all the facts laid out in the text and order them chronologically, using the third-person singular. As a result, they should come up with a more or less straight-line narrative of the principal events in the character's life, avoiding emotional coloring. The following example applies to the character of Ellida in The Lady from the Sea.

Ellida

- Grew up in a small seaside town called Skoldviken.
- Met a seafarer called Freeman and fell in love with him.
- Was engaged to Freeman, who left in a sea voyage.
- Lost traces of Freeman, married a doctor called Wangel and moved to another town, a small town by the fjords.
- Met Freeman again after many years, when he came back to claim her as his wife.
- Deliberated whether to break up her marriage to Wangel and return to the seaman.
- Confronted Freeman and ultimately chose to stay married to Wangel.

Activity 2. Character Bio (with Inferences)

Ask your actors to put together a profile of their character, using the first-person singular, this time by filling in the gaps of the script and *inferring* facts about the character's life. Have them start by asking and answering questions that might seem applicable, and then create a more detailed account of things that the playwright may have left out. A character's bio can include the basics (age, social/family/economic/educational status, profession, etc.), but also information that concerns hobbies, secret preferences, or undeclared ambitions. This "bio" can be enriched throughout the rehearsals. Include any of the following:

- Name;
- Age;

- Family status (spouse/children/parents/siblings);
- Relatives, friends, neighbors, acquaintances, love affairs;
- Profession;
- Family background and childhood;
- City of origin and city of residence;
- Daily habits;
- Hobbies;
- Any secrets;
- Any fears, anxieties, etc.

Activity 3. A Day in the Life of the Character

A useful improvisational exercise is describing a typical day in the life of the character, using the first-person singular. Depending on what you decide to include in your account, an emphasis on this or that aspect of the play can become apparent. Focusing on the character's daily routine, you will gradually be able to imagine elements that you were not formerly aware of and that can further add to the character's psychological portrait. The following is an attempt to describe Willy Loman's typical day:

Example: "Every morning I get up around 6.30. The first thing I do after brushing my teeth and having breakfast is to go out in the back garden and check on the seeds I planted a few weeks ago. I like stopping by the children's room and hearing Happy snore. Linda usually waits for me in the kitchen. Once again, I realize that I still haven't made the monthly payment for the fridge. I eat slowly because I feel drained and try to avoid the inevitable: to get up, start my car, and travel all those miles to try and sell things that nobody wants to buy."

Activity 4. Diary

An alternative to the previous exercise is going through the scenes of the play, keeping a diary that records everything that happens from the point of view of the character. This may, for example, help determine how differently Willy and Linda experience the events of the day.

In the scene where Willy confesses to Linda the feelings of inferiority he has recently experienced at work, this exercise could potentially unveil two different facets of the problem.

Willy's version

"This morning I finally spoke to Linda about what's happening at work. I tried to make her see that although I'm really trying, people still find me funny. I'm sure Linda knows that and just feels sorry for me. Of course, this is just a passing thing, and I must tell her not to worry too much. She must know how good I am and how I'll do great in the end. I'm Willy Loman, and I've always been liked."

Linda's version

"This morning Willy and I finally talked. He said things aren't good at work. He even said everyone's laughing at him. I don't know what I can do to help. He should really get a grip on reality. Things are no longer the way they used to be, and he still doesn't see that. He should be careful not to talk too much. Not to talk about himself all the time. To listen more. If only I could tell him that. But I know he wouldn't understand."

Activity 5. Character Lists

In your play of choice, have your actors study all the character information—direct or indirect—in the script. Reading closely, they should:

- Compile a list of things that character says about him/herself.

- Compile a list of things that all the other characters say about him/her.

- Compile a list of things that the actor instinctively feels the character is, taking into account what he/she says as opposed to what he/she does.

Activity 6. Past, Present, and Future

Have your actors do a background check on the character's past and compare it to their circumstances at present, considering the character's objectives and super-objective throughout the play.

Practice 2. Physicalizing Character

The following exercises can be applied while the actor approaches character physically—whether independently, as a single dramatic entity, or in connection to the rest of the characters in the play.

Activity I. Character Status

In *The Lady from the Sea,* pay particular attention to the Ellida-Stranger encounters in Acts III and V. On a scale of 1–10, how would you rate their character status at the end of Act III and the end of Act V, and why? Give your actors an explicit action, a movement, and a specific placement in space that would reflect their characters' higher or lower status in relation to each other. Make sure to incorporate any physical adjustments when a change in status occurs.

Activity 2. Character Status in Tragedy

Apply the previous exercise to the Oedipus-Tiresias scene of *Oedipus Rex.* Note how Oedipus' status decreases dramatically from a position of power (lines 300–304) to that of being a suspect (lines 440–446). As a director, how do you intend to portray this change physically?

Activity 3. Still Image

Divide your company into different groups. In your play of choice, have the actors express the predominant dramatic event of a key scene in a still image, physicalizing the posture, gesture, and status of each character. Ask the rest of the group to guess which part of the scene this image represents. Then, ask the actors to animate the picture and move the story to its conclusion.

Practice 3. Unit-ing and Action-ing

Fundamental strategies of text analysis, unit-ing and action-ing are used by a large number of directors in different variations and with different levels of emphasis. What follows is a common form of breaking down the script into units and determining the action that reveals the character's objectives and obstacles in each unit.

Have your actors read out loud a central scene in your play of choice.

Ask them to take turns reporting the events of the scene in their own words.

Work together with them to "unit" the scene.

Each actor must come up with a representative title for each unit—collecting unit titles functions as a way of crystallizing the interpretation of the scene in total.

Each actor should also select a specific character action for their character and share it with the group.

You and the actors can make suggestions for the character's *business*, the actual activities that put into physical practice the spirit of the action. Justify your choices, especially when they differ from what the playwright has suggested.

Practice 4. Character and Space

Actors need time to explore the setting of the play physically. The following two exercises are about walking through the rehearsal space and interacting—in character—with the rest of the performers. It is a basic improvisational technique that helps performers find their bearings in the world of the play.

Activity 1. Feeling at Home

As soon as the set is delivered into the theatre space, introduce it to your company, explaining its exact function and any changes that may have occurred in the original design. Let the actors move about the playing area, first as performers and then in character, exploring their position in it. After they have spent some time walking around, have them consider the following questions:

- How do I (how does my character) connect to this space?
- Is this my home? Workplace? A strange, new environment?
- Where do I enter? Where do I exit?
- Are there any particularly tricky spots to which I should pay extra attention?
- What is the energy of the space in each scene?
- Who else is in the space with me?
- If this is an open-air space, how public is it?

Activity 2. Between the Scenes

Have your actors imagine where their characters are at the moment physically but also mentally and ask them to think about what these characters do when they are not in the scene.

- Where exactly do they go when they exit the scene?
- Are they alone or do they interact with other characters who are not in the scene either?
- What goes on in their life before they reappear in the spotlight?

Give them some time to consider a rough plan for each act or scene and then have them write a paragraph about their actors' whereabouts and movements between scenes.

Practice 5. Improvising

Improvisation exercises are fundamental to restoring vitality to a scene, especially when it feels over-rehearsed and tired. They also help bridge the gap between character and self. Controlling the quality and duration of improvising can keep it tight and constructive.

Midway through rehearsals, have your actors run a scene in their own words and encourage them to use whichever style or register comes natural to them, as characters. They can even go through the script, line by line, and paraphrase everything. Such exercise can unblock parts of the text that for some reason continue to remain opaque. If language fails to communicate the meaning of the phrase, you can ask the actors to improvise a especially complex bit of a dialogue using movement only. If the energy sags and the exercise appears to have reached a dead end, you should either gear it toward a new focus and a point to explore or have the actors return to their text and let the discoveries of improvisation inform their acting.

Practice 6. Movement

Improvising with different forms of movement is probably the most inventive way for actors to explore the play and their role physically. They can also interact—in character—with the rest of the performers. Encourage the group to apply surprising detail to their movement to make it look and feel more authentic.

Activity 1. Variations in Walking

To experiment with variations in the shape and rhythm of movement, ask your actors to express the following situations physically:

- Returning home after having been fired from your job.
- Walking to a new and exciting romantic date.
- Walking to the doctor's office to get the results of an important medical test.
- Returning home after a long and exhausting day at work.
- Walking toward the departure gate at the airport after saying goodbye to your family and moving to another country.
- Waiting at the arrivals gate at the airport to pick up your son after an absence of several years.

Activity 2. Physicalizing Emotional States

Divide your actors into groups of four to five, and ask them to create with movement a silent scene, where one of the following emotional states prevails:

- Excitement;
- Rage;
- Grief;
- Relief;
- Lack of motivation.

Directions from and for Directors

Directions for Actors

Clearly, a touchstone of directing is supporting the actor in the effort to balance between imagination and control. Talent and intuition are difficult, if not impossible, to instill. However, inspiring performers to overcome hard-set inhibitions and aim for a break-through is well worth any agonies or losses incurred along the way. In tune with the title of the book, the closing chapter will conclude with some basic directions—from directors to actors but also from directors to themselves.

Although most directors tend to be consistent in their preferences when it comes to the kind of actors they like to work with, depending on the distinctive style and the aesthetic, practical, or commercial demands of the production, they will probably look for special actor qualities or skills. A strong background in physical theatre, for instance, will be of more benefit to a devised theatre project than to a nineteenth-century drawing-room drama staged realistically. Being experienced in the American Method will serve little in musical theatre if the actor's voice is untrained. In this sense, adjusting your director's hierarchies when casting is both healthy and sensible.

Here is a list of actor skills that directors commonly look for:

Directors-Actors: What directors want [from the actor]

- A level of experience;
- Solid technique;
- Voice training;
- Ability to enunciate and to project;

- Physical dexterity and versatility;
- Team player spirit, ability to work as an ensemble member;
- Presence onstage;
- Originality;
- Intuition and spontaneity;
- Eagerness to experiment;
- Physical discipline and control.

Similarly, here is an attempt to put together some basic actor needs that a director should cater for:

Actors-Directors: What actors need [from the director]

- An understanding of what the director is trying to achieve, in other words, a clear vision.
- Detailed guidance through the text.
- A joined exploration of the character but also, permission to get to know the character freely, without constant interference in the actor's process.
- A shared analysis of actions and objectives.
- Permission to provide a truthful, imaginative, original "take" on the character, which will be simultaneously unique to the actor and exciting to the audience.
- Time to understand what the character wants.
- Time to understand the character's external obstacles and inner conflicts.
- Permission to experiment with different ways of embodying character physically.
- Time to create an inventory of personality traits that reveal the character's attitudes, habits, assumptions, and prejudices.
- Time to examine the meaning of each line of text and try different ways of delivery.
- Help with determining how one character relates to the other characters in the play.
- Analysis of all the information that the text provides about a character: what characters say about themselves and what is said about them.

And, finally, here is some advice that a director should not hesitate to impart, given that every actor likes to feel invariably safe, free, independent, supported, excited, and empowered:

Directors-Actors: What directors should ask [of the actor]

- Connect. Concentrate. Communicate.
- Be brave.
- Be a meticulous reader. Know your text.
- Imagine. Daydream. Create your character's world.
- Keep learning. Keep improving your mind with more ideas.
- Keep training your body and your voice. Work out. Warm up before rehearsal and performance.
- Never hesitate to ask. Claim clarifications, where needed.
- Do your homework. Come to rehearsals prepared. Know your lines when you're expected to.
- Do more than what is expected of you. More of what you expect from yourself. Be daring.
- Be a good collaborator. Listen to your director and your fellow actors. Listen to your character, without judgment.
- Come to rehearsal on time. Shake off your private self as you walk into the room.
- Contain but do not suppress your feelings when things are not working. Ask for help.
- Be patient with yourself and your character; you two have only just met.
- Provide alternatives when the director is not satisfied.
- Try things out without nagging, even if you are vehemently opposed to them.
- Be generous to your fellow actors onstage. Be mindful of upstaging them and stealing focus.
- Be caring toward your character: you may think you're very different, but you are responsible for making the two of you meet.
- Don't refuse to improvise when you're asked to.
- Experiment and make mistakes. That's what rehearsals are for.
- Have fun making yourself look and sound ridiculous in rehearsal.
- Repeat what you feel you've done right.
- Repeat what your director says you've done right.
- Accept the fact that some rehearsals bring little result.
- Be kind to your directors—they're human beings too and often just as afraid as you are.
- Try the difficult thing. Make yourself bolder. Try the other door. Travel the "road not taken."
- Engage. Don't simply take part.
- Surrender, don't resist.
- Be brave. Be strong. Be vulnerable.

Directions for Directors

As a director, you are responsible for the entire group, the whole production, but also for yourself. To be of better use to everyone, you should keep looking inward and be attentive to your company's voice but also alert to your own instincts. The following *directions for directors* are a few mental notes to which you can always revert when your own motivation slackens and working with the actors seems strenuous, fragile, or a standstill.

Notes to Oneself

PAY ATTENTION!

Watching and listening are priceless. So is being willing to evaluate what you have observed and finding useful and objective ways of letting the actor know what can be improved. A director-spectator will follow the actors at all times, but the quality of attention can vary according to the targets set for each rehearsal. You can focus on the details of specific movements, a premature entrance, a wrong placement onstage, or a particular line or piece of dialogue that is done too fast or too slow. However, sometimes it is also of advantage to allow your eyes and ears to wander over the full scene, without resting on any particular moment for too long. This will help you grasp its energy, rhythm, and emotional texture, and make adjustments where necessary.

> **THOUGHT**
>
> The director must instantly focus the actor's attention on any important discovery that enters a moment of rehearsal.

EXPECT MORE, BUT BE PATIENT!

> **THOUGHT**
>
> Directors should keep watch of their anxiety and train themselves to wait for the actor's moment of revelation, even if that seems to take too long. Imagination needs time to spread its roots, and rushing actors to achieving immediate results can be detrimental to their creativity and confidence.

How can you encourage your actors to transform? Invite them to respond to what is happening to them and be affected by any new knowledge or interaction this brings. Keep pushing for the surprises that come with being open and connected, but trust actors to arrive at this vulnerable state naturally and with little pressure. Directing is (also) the art of (once again) balancing; this time, between faith and subtle soliciting.

CONTROL BAD HABITS!

Keeping an unrelenting eye on the actors' bad habits and fearlessly pointing them out as soon as they are noticed is one of your most thankless, but in the end, also unavoidable and indispensable tasks. Such patterns include but are not limited to: emoting, body insecurity, lack of projection, an untrained voice, overindulging/overacting, tendency to mask other actors, and tendency to miss one's light spot. When actors feel uncomfortable with certain lines or movements, they will revert to familiar gestures or delivery styles. In a run-through, take notes about the habits to which your actors seem particularly attached. Watch out for:

- Excessive gesticulation;
- General movement along the stage (the actor won't stand still during a monologue);
- General anger;
- Becoming very quiet to the point of whispering (you can barely hear what they are saying);
- Becoming very loud during moments of dramatic tension;
- Illustrating the action;
- Grimacing;
- Reduced body, vocal, and speech control.

THOUGHT

Actors tend to fall back on familiar technique, unable or unwilling to give it up. Keep reminding them, for most of the times they are not even aware of it.

KEEP THE ACTOR ALIVE!

A director can ask the actors to sustain their energy and keep them aligned to their actions, from their initial entrance up to their final exit. Such guidance restores focus on what is immediately present. Concentrating on their fellow performers makes their interaction with the other characters in the play more spontaneous.

THOUGHT

If concentration and stamina fail, you can occasionally let the actor resort to technique—even if temporarily—to get through the rough patches.

GAUGE THE ACTORS' ENERGY AND RESTORE BELIEF!

> **THOUGHT**
>
> Through experience, you will learn to recognize the actors' different tides of energy in rehearsal. Give your company the necessary respite, if needed, and, reversely, intensify the work, when the spirit of discovery is high.

There are times when actors will feel disenchanted with the process and lose faith in what they are doing. In those moments, your job is to turn them back to the basic *Wh-questions*, revise ineffective actions, and ground them in the space of their environment through sharper blocking.

RESPECT THE PROCESS!

Some practitioners who come to directing through acting have a natural way of speaking to performers and are usually treated with less suspicion, at least initially. Others have a stronger background in dramaturgy and may have trouble addressing the ensemble in clear, understandable language—they tend to intellectualize, discussing *ideas* instead of *actions*, and abstract concepts rather than playable tasks. On the other hand, some directors find it difficult to accept that a "Method" actor needs "a moment" to "prepare," or, by the same token, that some actors will resist improvisation or find table work

> **THOUGHT**
>
> Both directors and actors must realize that whichever gate they enter the play from in terms of training, style, and personality, everyone is ultimately traveling to the same destination. Adjustment is key.

tedious. Share your progress and respect your actor's part in it. Learn to be patient: trust is won gradually.

GIVE HELPFUL NOTES!

Note giving is an essential phase of directing. There is a wide range of notes for different aspects of rehearsal, which can interrupt the run of a scene to offer solutions for immediate adjustment. There is also the full score of notes that the director gives at the end of a run-through. Technical notes mostly concern blocking (landing a perfect entrance or exit, staying lit or avoiding masking), volume (adjusting the levels of delivery and projecting), and rhythm (off pacing, responding erroneously to lighting or sound cues). Fundamental acting issues are ordinarily addressed at the feedback session that follows rehearsal. In general, it is useful to involve the whole company and listen to what the actors have to say about problems that must be worked on further and which you may have failed to notice. Sometimes notes should be given to an actor individually, especially when the issues that need to be addressed are not instantly redeemable, relating, for instance, to the lack of a particular skill or the inability to deliver, in general.

THOUGHT

Notes are necessary for an actor to improve an opaque moment. For that, they must be precise and, when necessary, also detailed. They are there to suggest alternatives and serve as an opportunity to fix problems that have been overlooked in a previous rehearsal or run-through.

LISTS TO ONESELF

In times of doubt or after a turbulent day in rehearsal, there may be some value in putting down on paper things that might need to be reworked or addressed even more meticulously. You can revisit the fundamental principles of your craft and have faith that, one way or another, they will continue to infuse your practice.

Director's "To Do List"

- Imagining the world of the play, together with the actor;
- Offering helpful, playable alternatives, when an actor feels stuck;
- Being specific, concise, and passionate;
- Avoiding definitive and prescriptive character statements, which tend to close the play down;
- Encouraging improvisation when the actor's connection to the text and the character is weak or missing entirely;
- Bringing in helpful research in rehearsal;
- Asking clarifying questions;
- Asking the actor to project, when inaudible;
- Paying attention to masking issues;

- Giving actors specific physical tasks and prompts;
- Challenging with unexpected requests and raising the stakes in the scene;
- Scrutinizing alternatives for motivations and actions;
- Encouraging group warm-ups at the beginning of rehearsal;
- Listening to actors' suggestions;
- Being alert to any sources of tension in the room;
- Pointing out the actor's bad habits and mannerisms;
- Being sensitive to the company's physical exhaustion;
- Being sensitive to the company's emotional state;
- Acknowledging any break-through the actor has had;
- Pointing out when an actor is overacting;
- Pointing out inconsistencies in movement or line delivery;
- Pointing out mistakes (we tend to learn from them!);
- Containing an overly eager actor;
- Asking the actor to stay in the moment and not play the whole scene at once;
- Showing patience when an actor is having a hard time with a particular scene, a speech, or a physical position;
- Interrupting the scene when an actor is feeling uncomfortable or loses his or her concentration;
- Watching out for the motivation that propels each movement;
- Showing, when explaining fails;
- Always mentioning some positive things, however small, during feedback;
- Being present, being available;
- Motivating, explaining, encouraging, listening, expecting, waiting, giving, learning to receive, investing, and surrendering.

And, finally, by the same token,

Director's "Not to Do" List

- Giving general feedback rather than concrete suggestions;
- Ignoring recurrent problems in rehearsal;
- Being too cerebral, abstract, or intellectual when talking to actors;
- Refusing to listen to actors' suggestions;

- Refusing to reconsider a blocking choice;
- Dismissing tensions among actors as insignificant;
- Giving line readings;
- Giving feedback at inopportune moments;
- Not offering detailed feedback after run-throughs;
- Being too eager to please the actor by always giving overly positive notes;
- Not paying attention to the actors' discoveries;
- Discouraging the group after a poor run-through;
- Being too complacent;
- Over-complimenting;
- Giving technical notes to an actor who works from a psychological base (from "inside-out");
- Allowing text analysis to digress into a chaotic guesswork or chit-chat;
- Intimidating inexperienced actors;
- Being inflexible and arrogant;
- Being impatient for instant results.

The Director as Spectator, or Else, Postproduction Blues

How can a director ever go back to being an innocent spectator who watches the show as if for the first time? Is it still possible to retain in rehearsal the freshness of an original response and become the audience's eyes and ears, fearlessly pointing out to the actor those moments when he or she is neither heard nor seen? No matter how strong the chimerical nature of a character's private world is—in many productions, it is also reinforced by the imaginary fourth wall—the actors still need to maintain an engaged communication with the audience, and you should be there to make it happen.

Essentially, the director communicates to the audience a story (the play) through a concept (a form). Assuming another person's identity, actors come onstage prepared to take a leap into the void. Leaving a part of themselves behind, they disengage from their private reality—if only for a little while—to fully enter that liminal, ephemeral space of "meeting the character" in front of a group of expectant strangers. In the end, the absolute test of the directors' and actors' entire period of preparation, rehearsal time, and actual performance is the audience's response to what it sees and what it hears. Few spectators are concerned with tracing the process behind the product. Most crave to experience an effortless performance of a fluid and stirring story, irrespective of the methodology that has been applied to realize it. All the audience perceives is the actor in performance. Choosing to accept the constitutional illusion of the stage world and of character, it does not know, nor should it care about the work that has gone into the production.

For a director, opening night is a bit like sending your young kids off to school for the first time. The crisis of abandoning the safety of home (the rehearsal room) to jump into an open, precarious condition (the performance) is exciting, but no doubt also very scary. What kind of support and encouragement can you give your actors to see them out into the world? What about this empty feeling in the stomach as soon as you realize that your job is done?

Cutting the umbilical cord is primarily a physical act. The emotional connection will always be there, defining every aspect of the parent-child relationship. On your end, you will eventually learn to accept the inevitable reality that as your children continue to grow, they will continue to be less and less dependent on you. They may feel less inclined to spend time with their mom and dad, being busy making new friends and discovering the world unhampered by nagging demands and admonitions. Just as parents learn to contain their anxiety when handing over a toddler to a kindergarten for the first time, so must you also concede to taking the back seat—literally, for few directors can brave watching their performances from the front rows of the auditorium—and let the actor make a splash. All the support, love, the comforting awareness that you have done the best that you could to create the circumstances for creativity are there, but now the child/actor is ready to open those wings and fly. Nothing can or should stop that from happening. Not even the knowledge that anything may happen along the way, that the first time away from home may not be as fulfilling as they may have wished, but that the guidance and the skills and the dreams you have instilled will hopefully mature and expand and spread out wide. Staying behind, you can only watch and enjoy. Your journey as a director may be more or less complete, but the adventure of performance is only just beginning.

WORKS CITED

Boenisch, Peter M. and Thomas Ostermeier. *The Theatre of Thomas Ostermeier.* London and New York: Routledge, 2016.

Delgado, Maria M. and Dan Rebellato, eds. *Contemporary European Theatre Directors.* London and New York: Routledge, 2010.

Fosse, Jon. *Plays One.* London: Oberon Books, 2002.

Herbert, Robert L., ed. 1964. *Modern Artists on Art.* New York: Dover Publications, 2000.

Hodge, Francis. 1971. *Play Directing. Analysis, Communication, and Style.* Fourth Edition. Englewood Cliffs, NJ: Prentice Hall, 1994.

Mamet, David. *True and False: Heresy and Common Sense for the Actor.* New York: Vintage, 1999.

Miller, Arthur. *Death of a Salesman.* 1949. New York: Penguin Books, 1986.

Panet, Brigit. *Essential Acting. A Practical Handbook for Actors, Teachers and Directors.* With Fiona McHardy. London: Routledge, 2009.

Zarrilli, Phillip. 1995. *Acting (Re)Considered: A Theoretical and Practical Guide.* London and New York: Routledge, 2002.